theatre & architecture

Theatre &
Series Editors: Jen Harvie and Dan Rebellato

Theatre&
Series Standing Order ISBN 978–0–230–20327–3

You can receive future titles in this series as they are published by placing a standing order. Please contact your bookseller or, in case of difficulty, write to us at the address below with your name and address, the title of the series and the ISBN quoted above.

Customer Services Department, Macmillan Distribution Ltd, Houndmills, Basingstoke, Hampshire, RG21 6XS, UK

theatre & architecture

Juliet Rufford

 macmillan education palgrave

First published 2015 by
PALGRAVE

Palgrave in the UK is an imprint of Macmillan Publishers Limited,
registered in England, company number 785998, of 4 Crinan Street, London N1 9XW.

Palgrave Macmillan in the US is a division of St Martin's Press LLC,
175 Fifth Avenue, New York, NY 10010.

Palgrave is a global imprint of the above companies and is represented
throughout the world.

Palgrave® and Macmillan® are registered trademarks in the United States,
the United Kingdom, Europe and other countries.

ISBN: 978–0–230–21872–7 paperback

This book is printed on paper suitable for recycling and made from fully
managed and sustained forest sources. Logging, pulping and manufacturing
processes are expected to conform to the environmental regulations of the
country of origin.

A catalogue record for this book is available from the British Library.

A catalog record for this book is available from the Library of Congress.

Printed in China

contents

For Phoebe, Matteo and Luca

series editors' preface

The theatre is everywhere, from entertainment districts to the fringes, from the rituals of government to the ceremony of the courtroom, from the spectacle of the sporting arena to the theatres of war. Across these many forms stretches a theatrical continuum through which cultures both assert and question themselves.

Theatre has been around for thousands of years, and the ways we study it have changed decisively. It's no longer enough to limit our attention to the canon of Western dramatic literature. Theatre has taken its place within a broad spectrum of performance, connecting it with the wider forces of ritual and revolt that thread through so many spheres of human culture. In turn, this has helped make connections across disciplines; over the past fifty years, theatre and performance have been deployed as key metaphors and practices with which to rethink gender, economics, war, language, the fine arts, culture and one's sense of self.

Theatre & is a long series of short books which hopes to capture the restless interdisciplinary energy of theatre and performance. Each book explores connections between theatre and some aspect of the wider world, asking how the theatre might illuminate the world and how the world might illuminate the theatre. Each book is written by a leading theatre scholar and represents the cutting edge of critical thinking in the discipline.

We have been mindful, however, that the philosophical and theoretical complexity of much contemporary academic writing can act as a barrier to a wider readership. A key aim for these books is that they should all be readable in one sitting by anyone with a curiosity about the subject. The books are challenging, pugnacious, visionary sometimes and, above all, clear. We hope you enjoy them.

Jen Harvie and Dan Rebellato

theatre & architecture

Introduction

An unlikely combination

In the early years of the twentieth century, in a commercial culture of insincerity, distracting scenery and overblown acting styles, the French theatre director Jacques Copeau vowed to rejuvenate the theatre by taking actors and directors through a professional training programme. Although nothing of the sort had ever existed before, Copeau decided to open an academy, which would act in tandem with his Théâtre du Vieux-Colombier. His modest but significant undertaking became an institutional reality in December 1921, when a select number of students (perhaps, a little nervous) entered the doors of 9 Rue du Cherche-Midi, on Paris's Left Bank. Anyone who knew Copeau's energetic, risk-taking personality might have been prepared for the novelty and breadth of classes on offer: his curriculum design ranged from prosody and poetic technique to stagecraft, voice-work, improvisation, dance and even acrobatics (Maurice Kurtz, *Jacques Copeau: Biography of a Theatre*, 1999; John Rudlin, *Jacques Copeau*, 1986; Mark Evans, *Jacques Copeau*, 2006). But who would have guessed there would be an entire module on architecture?

For Copeau, architecture is the most fundamental and consistently overlooked aspect of theatre. In fact, he places architecture at the heart of theatre aesthetics, dramaturgy and genre since, as he puts it, 'a given dramatic conception postulates a certain stage design and just as much or even more: a given stage architecture calls forth, demands and gives rise to a certain dramatic conception and style of presentation [so that] it is difficult to say which is responsible for the formation of a particular style, the form of the drama or the form of the theatre' (*Copeau: Texts on Theatre*, 1990, p. 88). In Copeau's view, architecture does not simply contain drama but *produces* it by co-creating its meanings, conventions and aesthetics.

We can test his thesis by picking a place and time in history and picturing both the built form and the drama of that theatrical moment. By analysing the defining features of a given dramatic genre and the acting style most commonly associated with it in terms of the architecture of the auditorium in which it developed, we get a powerful sense of the way that architecture conditions and constructs elements of theatre. For instance, in Japanese Kabuki theatres, the *hanamichi* – the platform that connects the stage to the back of the auditorium by passing through the audience – highlights entrances and exits and supports the tradition whereby actors stop to explain their roles to the audience before coming on. The *hanamichi* forms a physical and metatheatrical passage between the realms of fiction and reality, providing an important opportunity for audiences to witness a transition – from actor to character – that, in Western proscenium-arch theatre, would take place, unseen, in the wings.

Other examples from around the world show how theatrical meaning, aesthetics and acting styles have been tied to theatre architecture from the earliest times to the present. The huge size of the ancient Greek amphitheatre demanded large gestural acting. By contrast, the smaller Elizabethan amphitheatre, with its thrust stage and warm materials (wood, thatch and lathe), created an intimate experience, although playwrights could still exploit the theatre's 'cosmic' polygonal shape to express the idea that 'all the world's a stage' and that the wooden O is the world, or globe, in microcosm (Shakespeare, *As You Like It*, II.vii.140). More recently, Lina Bo Bardi's 1984 refit of the Teatro Oficina in São Paulo, Brazil, as a scaffolding and glass alley-way, linking two pedestrian areas of the Bexiga neighbourhood at either end of its nine-by-fifty-metre site, infuses each production with the energy of the street.

Even theatre that is ostensibly unconcerned with architecture is powerfully conditioned by it nonetheless. Architecture articulates space, giving it a particular feel. Staging a performance is about acting in architecture: it is a practice that demands we pay attention to distance, scale, style, person-to-volume ratio and the immaterial architectures of light, heat and sound. In *A Short History of Western Performance Space* (2003), David Wiles compares the white cube art gallery and the theatrical black box studio, arguing that 'analysts of theatre have been slower than analysts of modern art to perceive how far meaning is a function of space' (p. 258). The stakes are especially high in relation to black box theatres because, as Wiles explains, the myth of their neutrality has been so convincing. But the relationship between architectural space and theatrical meaning applies to every type of theatre.

We can see this in two productions of the same play – Sarah Kane's *4.48 Psychosis* – staged within a year at the same venue (London's Royal Court theatre) by the same director–designer team: James Macdonald and Jeremy Herbert. The 2000 première was in the Court's Theatre Upstairs, a low-ceilinged studio, where the tiny proportions of the room and steep rake of the seats were accentuated by Herbert's decision to hang an enormous mirror at a forty-five-degree angle to the acting area. This cramped arrangement brought out the sense of being trapped inside Kane's world. Sitting so close to the work, and seeing the actors and the other spectators reflected above and before me, I found the play visceral, oppressive and painfully intimate. When I returned the following year, to see it revived in the Theatre Downstairs, not only did the larger proscenium-arch space alter my sense of the play by framing its action as distinct and separate from the world of the spectator but also the style of the auditorium re-positioned the work's meanings. A feeling of luxury fills this (refurbished)

4

nineteenth-century room. With its deep Rothko reds, rich browns and soft blacks, its soothing leather seats and the fading splendour of the intricate mouldings that festooned its balconies in days gone by, it evokes the urbane atmosphere of a private members' club. Against this, the voices of Kane's mental health patients floated coldly distant.

We might take things one step further than Copeau and ask questions that are not limited to how we read the staged events but extend to include audience behaviours and the social experience of theatre-going. For instance, by turning our attention to our imaginary audience, we could ask how the features of architectural space work to establish a certain social code. I will take Richard Wagner's Bayreuther Festspielhaus (1876), designed by Otto Brückwald under the guidance of Karl Brandt, because this theatre allows me to compare the architectural and social codes of two major phases of European performance: the baroque and the modern.

In stark contrast to the horseshoe-shaped opera houses of the late sixteenth to mid-nineteenth centuries, where auditorium and stage were bathed in shared lighting and the walls were peopled with audience members who often talked, flirted with one another and cast their gaze over other spectators, the Bayreuther Festspielhaus provided a highly concentrated experience. Wagner's audience sat in a single fan of seats with clear sightlines to the stage. Staggered sidewalls replaced the private boxes of a previous era and optically shortened the distance between the auditorium and the acting area, channelling viewpoints forwards.

But perhaps the most significant change of all was that the auditorium lights were turned down as the orchestra struck up the opening notes of Wagner's *Der Ring des Nibelungen* (*The Ring*). In the dark, the sights and sounds of the auditorium were stilled. It was as if architecture and audience had disappeared and the only thing in existence at that moment was the drama unfolding on the stage. If you recognise this scenario, where the lowering of the house lights is your cue to stop chatting to your neighbour and turn your attention to the stage, it is because the Bayreuther Festspielhaus is the prototype of the modern Western auditorium, establishing through its seating layout and through its skilful use of light the model of 'correct' behaviour that has conditioned experiences of theatre-going from that time until today.

Despite some daring architectural experimentation by modern and contemporary theatre-makers, including members of the European avant-gardes and the American neo-avant-gardes, Copeau's stress on the primacy of architecture remains surprising to most drama students. Few university drama courses offer the chance to study performance in relation to theatre architecture – or even teach the basic stage types – although many appreciate the need for classes on scenography and technical theatre. For their part, theatre architects of the past hundred years have often failed to meet the needs of performers, and a mutual suspicion has grown up between theatre folk and design professionals. Relations seem to have hit an all-time low around the building of Britain's National Theatre by Denys Lasdun in 1970s London, when the actor Albert Finney, on hearing

Peter Brook say that a theatre should be like a violin, its tone coming from its period and age, snorted: 'who'd build a violin out of fucking concrete?' (Richard Eyre, *National Service*, 2004, p. 44). How did relations between theatre and architecture get so bad?

In our recent history, theatre and architecture have come to be understood as polar opposites: theatre is a temporal form; architecture is a spatial practice. While theatre has always been considered as art, architecture is often classified as an applied science. If theatre sometimes battles criticism that it lacks solid purpose, architecture cannot avoid its life-or-death responsibility to make buildings that stand up. Whereas theatre deals with fiction, architecture is perceived to be real. If theatre can sometimes evade the market, architecture – if it wants to get built – has to cooperate with capital and power. Performance celebrates collaboration, experiment and group improvisation (even a traditionally scripted play will need the combined talents of dramatist, director, designer, actors and many others to make the transition from page to stage), yet many architects cling jealously to an ideal of solo authorship. Theatre conjures the transient and transgressive; architecture stands for durability and boundaries. Given such apparent dissimilarity, some people feel that these disciplines have little to say to, or to learn from, each other. One key assumption of this book is that understandings of theatre and architecture and of the relationship between them are historically and culturally contingent. Thus, the propositions listed above stem from particular developments or events in the history of each discipline and are not timeless or universal. Theatre and architecture are not always so dissimilar at all.

Challenging assumptions

Theatre *is* a temporal art but it is also one that signifies spatially. We have seen how architectural style, and the size, shape and materials of the theatre, condition theatrical meanings and aesthetics. Other ways in which space is central to theatrical meaning concern position and arrangement. One example of this can be seen in Sanskrit theatre, where action being played towards the back of the stage means that things are happening in the realm of the gods. Another example: in ancient Greece, the term 'chorus', which we still use to refer to the group of actors who witness the tragedy, derives from the Greek word for the dancing floor (*choros*). Hence, choreography is concerned not only with bodies and movement but with inscribing dance moves *across space* (see James Miller's *Measures of Wisdom: Cosmic Dance in Classical and Christian Antiquity*, 1986, for a full analysis of the links between choreography, *choros* and cosmos). By looking at where theatre takes place, and how it uses proxemics – distances between people – geometry, critical distancing, the framing of action and orientation in space, we may see aspects of its operation that have been hitherto obscured.

Theatre *can* be made inexpensively and with a minimum of outside interference (from business or state sponsorship) but it is economically embedded nonetheless. Prized, in recent decades, for its cultural capital – a kind of kudos used

8

as currency to leverage other types of capital – theatre's ties to the economy have deepened and become more complex. Urban developers now use theatre buildings to gentrify city centres and boost tourism through their 'regeneration' schemes (see Michael McKinnie's *City Stages*, 2007, for an account of how this global trend is playing out in Toronto). Given this state of affairs, it is vital that we keep in mind Alan Read's warning, in *Architecturally Speaking* (2000), neither to view the built environment as an 'amorphous urban backdrop setting' nor to 'valoris[e] space at the expense of the critical relations between temporality, built form and the performative dynamics of architecture within everyday life' (pp. 1–2). Since architecture has long existed at the nexus of real estate and urban development, it may provide insights into the forces linking theatre to urban planning, civic ideology and political economy.

Architecture *does* involve the application of scientific rules to building design (although much of the mathematics and physics of design, including calculating loads, levels of resistance or degrees of expansion, is now done by a structural engineer) but these rationalist principles were developed in nineteenth-century Europe in response to ideas of Enlightenment Reason. Elsewhere, architecture has often been practised according to social, spiritual or ideological precepts, which make it easier to discern its basis in human needs, thoughts and feelings. In the oldest surviving book on Western architecture, *De Architectura* (*c*.25 BCE), the Roman architect Vitruvius explains how architects need to combine knowledge of geometry, mathematics, human anatomy and astrology, bending architecture's rules where necessary and sometimes working intuitively. In south Asia, there are clear links between architecture, philosophy and religious ritual. For example, the *Natya Sastra*, the ancient Sanskrit theatre manual of India (attributed to the sage Bharata, and written between 200 BCE and 200 CE), makes extensive use of the theory of *rasa* – one-ness: a synthesis of artistic experience between perception and ethical action – in verse sections that describe the ritual construction of the playhouse. Like theatre, architecture is an amalgam of the rational and the felt. Indeed, theatre, as an art-form that is expressly concerned with human events and interactions, may help us to a better understanding of architecture's social and emotional dimensions.

Architecture *does* aspire to permanence – or, at least, it does in certain times, places and respects. Vitruvius lists durability, along with beauty and utility, as a core principle. Western architecture, as we learn from the nursery rhyme 'London Bridge', recommends stone over wood and clay. Traditional Japanese architecture, by contrast, aspires to lightness and uses wood and paper in place of heavier Western materials. Moreover, when Japanese buildings are preserved, it is not the fabric of the building that is protected (as in Western conservation) but the building *type*. The Naiku Shrine, in Ise, Japan, has been re-built in an act of ritual renewal some sixty-one times since it was first erected in the seventh century. This complicates notions of durability and duration in architecture, revealing one way in which a building may be thought to be ephemeral and to endure. If modern Western architecture finds this hard to comprehend, theatre, which frequently confronts this ephemerality/endurance paradox, might encourage architecture to think counter-intuitively about the culture of the built.

Look more theatrically at buildings in the Western world and you will see they are susceptible to the passage of time. Even when it does not succumb to fire, flood or war, architecture is death-bound, precarious. Buildings breathe and sigh, expand and contract, grow upwards and outwards (through extensions and conversions). Their outer appearance changes as they age, their skin becomes weathered, they groan and crack, and, eventually, they die. I am anthropomorphising built form – endowing it with human characteristics – but you take my point? We may imagine that a building, once complete, stays put. The reality is that it exists in a subtle state of flux. As Stewart Brand reminds us, in his book *How Buildings Learn: What Happens After They're Built* (1994), a '"building" is always building and re-building. The idea is crystalline; the fact is fluid' (p. 2). Architecture has a much longer duration than performance. It is as if it takes place in a parallel universe, where everything moves far more slowly than in the hyper-speedy realm of theatre. But architecture is itself a species of performer.

This short book aims to get beyond common prejudices and binary oppositions to see that theatre and architecture are multi-faceted and complex, and so, too, is any relationship between them. The fact that these disciplines share important overlaps of concern – including a focus on the human body, time and duration, spatiality and sociality, truth and fiction, structure and expression, and much else besides – is what enables us to compare them. However, I argue that their differences are of equal use in enabling new modes of knowledge to emerge, transforming each subject and set of practices. Next, some definitions and, then, an outline of the book.

Expanded fields, inter-disciplinary dialogues

The term 'theatre' as it is used throughout this book is broadly conceived. I use it to refer to the text-based theatre of all ages as well as a host of devised performance practices, including physical theatre, site-specific performance, installation work, soundwalks and dance-theatre. In expanding my notion of theatre, I am drawing on the insights of performance studies – a broad-based and inclusive field, which refuses to set theatrical performance above or apart from a wide variety of other artistic and social performances, rituals, acts of protest and resistance, and which views all performance within its cultural context. I also use an expanded definition of architecture as both the process and product of building design. Architecture involves a large range of considerations, from poetics and planning, symbolism and structure, to health and safety legislation and logistics of use. It is about the thoughtful design of space from the macro-level of urban design and landscape architecture to the micro-level of construction detailing and furniture design. Architecture, finally, is about the sculpting of space and the organisation of the environments in which we live and act – and which act upon us – through the use of light, materials, technology, texture and sound.

In what follows, I extrapolate from Copeau to argue that theatre and architecture are caught up in an interrogative aesthetics, one that uses the ruptures between them as much as their points of convergence to explore their signature dilemmas, the affordances and limitations of each. The book is divided into two main parts. In Part One: On Architecture, I discuss two terms ('mimesis' and 'performativity') that are closely related to theatre but are contentious when applied to architecture. I show how the former provides exciting opportunities for an architecture that seeks to enact different meanings for its users, and I argue that the latter, considered as an architectural *process*, might make use of the tools of performance to create alternative architectural performativities. In Part Two: On Theatre, I trace architecture's historical role in producing theatrical meaning; I show how early twentieth-century theatre-makers disrupted one order – that of the illusionist prosceniumarch stage – to establish other, more radical uses of architecture and how contemporary experiments use architecture to debunk myths that play out within, and extend beyond, the theatre. The book ends with an argument for the tectonic – the poetics of architectural construction – as a potentially valuable means of analysing and making theatre. Throughout, I question some of the assumptions we make about discrete disciplinary processes, and I reassess relationships between theatre, architecture and world. In working through these issues, I have been less interested in

13

the history of theatre architecture than I have been eager to know how theatre and architecture each unmask and re-negotiate defining features of the other. Consequently, this is not a book on theatre architecture (although I engage with examples of theatre architecture where this feels pertinent, I challenge theatre-makers and architects to think deeply about what a theatre building could be like, and I provide a list of books on theatre architecture in my 'further reading' section). This is a book about how theatre *and* architecture as disciplines and inter-disciplines act on one another in ways that might prove critically and artistically generative.

part one: on architecture

Architecture and mimesis

Situating architecture

Arguments about the nature of architecture are as old as architecture itself. To the extent that architecture is based upon geometry and mathematics, the Athenian philosopher Plato (c.424–347 BCE) sees it as a 'real thing', concerned with eternal forms, philosophical concepts and mathematical proofs that are discovered in nature and always hold true. Architecture is an art (what is real about it is not the building *per se* but the forms and ideas which give rise to it), but it is an art – unlike the imitative arts of drama, literature and painting, which copy or re-present nature at a further remove from reality – that has a powerful claim to truth. Today, many theorists argue that, apart from figurative additions to built form, architecture concerns spatial design and not imitative or 'mimetic' representation. Architects, according to this viewpoint, do not disclose an imaginary world; they add real productions to the real world.

However, the roots for understanding architecture as representational can also be traced to ancient Greece and Rome, where the language of the Classical orders – architectural styles identifiable by their unique proportions and characteristic details – expressed particular moods and cultural values and even suggested different human body types. Proponents of this view claim that temples dedicated to Mars, Hercules and Minerva were built in the Doric order – a plain-looking order with sturdy columns – because this was thought to represent the dignity and might of these divinities. Temples to Venus were built according to the more intricately decorated Corinthian order, the slender columns of which conveyed something of the goddess's gentle, 'feminine' nature, as well as the elegance and beauty of her physical form.

Another viewpoint holds that architecture is situated somewhere between the symbolic and the real. On the one hand, the fact that 'architect' derives from the ancient Greek word meaning 'chief builder' signals architecture's basis in construction. On the other, architecture is thought to possess poetic and aspirational qualities that transcend the pragmatism of building and imbue built form with meaning. Tectonics, a concept that focuses on structural force, technology, craft and form but ties these constructional concerns to symbolism, suggests a synthesis between architecture as real thing and architecture as representation. Yet it distinguishes architecture from visuospatial practices such as scenography – the design of performance environments – that create artistic impressions by mimicking the real. (Scenography, which encompasses set design, was established in the mid-sixteenth century when the architect Sebastiano Serlio first transferred principles he was using for the design of theatres to the stage itself. Although it is the natural child of architecture, scenography is part of theatre's 'make believe'.)

Kenneth Frampton, who reignited this debate in 'Rappel à l'Ordre: The Case for the Tectonic' (1990), uses philosopher Martin Heidegger's distinction between a 'thing' (real) and a 'sign' (indication of the real) to insist that 'building is ontological rather than representational in character and that built form is a presence rather than something standing for an absence' (p. 23; see also Heidegger, 'Building Dwelling Thinking', 1954). For Frampton, architecture's defining characteristics are its materiality, its relationship to topography and corporeality, and the charged relationship that should exist between the formal, structural and symbolic aspects of the work. But he questions the capacity of contemporary architecture practice to fully attend to the tectonic and to explore the expressive potential of structure and constructional technique in today's built projects. In particular, he takes issue with a growing culture of spectacle and representation, which he claims reduces architecture to scenography.

The reason Frampton wants to distance architecture from mimetic arts, and from scenography in particular, is that, historically, the tendency towards visual effects in architecture has coincided with an emphasis on architecture as commodity. Whereas Western architects from antiquity to the Renaissance practised their craft according to ethical principles (chiefly, decorum – propriety or appropriateness in the cultural context), the ideological and social values that emerged during the seventeenth century led later architects to think in terms of power, money and notions of display. From the mid-eighteenth century onwards, architects working in Europe signalled the social status of private property owners through their designs. Decorum elided into décor as a scenographic emphasis on appearances (including in the social sense) eclipsed architecture's structural and material probity.

I have a lot of sympathy with Frampton's suspicion of surface spectacle and I share his commitment to questioning how architecture today can exploit space and form, materials, construction and technology in order to resist what the Marxist cultural theorist Fredric Jameson terms the culture of late capital – the fusion of economic and cultural sensibilities that is currently giving rise to a global culture of media capitalism (*Postmodernism, or, the Cultural Logic of Late Capitalism*, 1991, pp. xviii–xxi). However, I believe scenography can hold out critical possibilities for architecture and that discrimination against mimetic art-forms is preventing a dialogue about how a representational architecture might work as cultural critique – as plenty of good theatre and theatre design does.

To give just one brief example of a critical scenographic practice, we might look at Dorita Hannah's design for a production of *Henry 8: A Sexual Sermon* devised, in 1992, by Theatre at Large and presented, in 1994, in Taki Rua's black box theatre in Wellington, New Zealand. Here, scenography exceeded its role in co-creating, and commenting on, the fictional world of performance to mount an architectural intervention. At the level of the play and its meanings (where you would expect scenography to operate), Hannah highlighted every scuff, scratch and mark on the walls with white paint and then applied layers of flaking black paper to them; the walls were then brushed with whitewash to turn them into blistering, sweating surfaces. Her idea was to 'reference the corrupt regime of Henry VIII, a syphilitic king who carved a smooth white swathe through the dark, diseased space in which the audience sat like members of his court, reminding us that, as onlookers, we are always complicit with history's events' ('Black Box / Black Wi(n)dow: Architecture of the Void', 2008). At the level of the (real) theatre space, Hannah's deliberate exacerbation of scuff-marks and other small imperfections in the otherwise pristine 'empty' space of the studio argued against the myth of black box neutrality by representing the wear and tear of human usage. The intervention thus critiqued residual attitudes in theatre and architecture that treat built form as a dumb container. By gesturing to the patterns of inhabitation and use that start scoring the surface of a building the minute that people begin to interact with it, it insisted that the theatre building – and, by extension, all architecture – is live, and that its spaces are socially produced.

The fact that this project raises questions that have a relevance and urgency beyond the theatre and this one particular production suggests to me that architects might make effective use of scenography across a wide range of typologies. But I am also interested in ways that architecture itself may be mimetic. Before I take this further, I want to raise the question of how one defines mimesis, because Frampton is right that some sort of mimesis, however banal, is at work in the ironic visual gags of postmodernism (e.g. in Charles Moore's Piazza d'Italia, New Orleans, 1978, or in Philip Johnson's decision to top his AT&T Tower, New York, 1984, with an ornamental pediment that looks like a piece of Chippendale furniture). And it is at work in a lot of the shallowly spectacular architectural projects of the twenty-first century. If we are going to try to find ways in which mimesis in architecture might promote a questioning of societal norms and prevailing ideas about reality, we will want to distinguish some understandings and manifestations of mimesis from others.

In contrast to narrow definitions of mimesis as an imitation of appearances (e.g. Plato or Heidegger), some philosophers argue that mimesis is neither exclusively visual nor passively imitative. These thinkers see it as active, transformative and revelatory. Plato's student Aristotle, who discusses mimesis in his *Poetics* (*c*.330 BCE), believes it is a fundamental process through which we mediate and learn about our world. This understanding shifts, in parts of seventeenth- and early eighteenth-century Europe, to embrace interior, emotive and subjective representations as well as representations of events and objects outside ourselves. Later still, Heidegger's contemporary Theodor Adorno defines mimetic activity in relation to interpersonal relations and critical social practice. Below, I take a brief look at the work of three architectural historians – Louise Pelletier, Dalibor Vesely and Hilde Heynen – who see mimesis as advancing architecture's social, cultural or political dimensions.

Re-tooling character theory

Louise Pelletier, in her *Architecture in Words: Theatre, Language and the Sensuous Space of Architecture* (2006), explores how use of an expressive language in architecture might endow the discipline today with a keener social purpose. She examines the implications of character theory in architecture at the end of the Ancien Régime – the political, social and aristocratic system of France before the revolution of 1789. Famous architects of that time published competing treatises in which they stressed that 'character' inhered in architecture's active, expressive and/or anthropomorphic aspects and promoted the idea – in contrast to the strictly codified, apparently unambiguous meanings of the Classical orders – that a building could signal moral values and articulate its civic purpose in ways that allowed for subtle variations in interpretation.

Singling out the explicitly theatrical character theory of Nicolas Le Camus de Mézières (1721–89), an acclaimed architect and lesser-known playwright, Pelletier discusses Le Camus's claims that the 'essence of architecture is fictional and poetic' and that architecture can be an 'active component in social interactions' (pp. 1 and 155). As a product of a culture witnessing the rise of the bourgeois individual, Le Camus believed a large part of the aim of architecture was to portray the personality and social status of the client in built form. Like many other late eighteenth-century architects working in France, he achieved this by capturing an atmosphere or association in the space that was not wholly coincident with the space itself but was a mimesis or representation. For instance, the house of a serious-minded public figure might call for an architectural representation of solemnity and poise through the use of appropriate materials (e.g. marble, which could be seen as luxurious yet weighty) and proportions (e.g. wide staircases and spacious rooms, which are suggestive of grandeur). However, Le Camus was also committed to exploring the transformative social role of architecture and, in Pelletier's account, he saw architecture as a vital way of mediating the social, emotional, psychological and moral life of users because it is able to 'speak to the mind and move the soul' (p. 1).

Although Le Camus's major architectural treatise *The Genius of Architecture; or, The Analogy of That Art with Our Sensations* (1780) makes no explicit reference to the then-influential ideas of sensationalist philosophy – a branch of thought which holds that we learn things not only with our rational mind but also through our senses – its subtitle and much of its argument make clear his view that knowledge is acquired through sensory perception. For Le Camus, an architecture that excites the senses by making an impression on its users can not only stimulate delight in architecture but also awaken perception and lead to moral judgement. Because theatre in the late eighteenth century was the locus of public and social expression, and theatrical acting the model for social behaviours on the public 'stage', a mimetic architecture might transcend its materiality and become a site for people to re-negotiate shared values and ideals.

Paradoxically, Le Camus's view of architecture's public relevance was played out in his design for the *hôtel particulier* – the private townhouse designed for wealthy citizens of Paris and other major cities. (He had envisaged writing a second part to his treatise, which would deal with the design for public buildings, but this was never realised.) He approached the design for the *hôtel particulier* in terms of the plotting of a play, using both the distribution of rooms and a gradual increase in ornamentation as ways to create dramatic tension and enhance the visitor's experience of journeying through them. While the character of each room would have been immediately apparent to all who entered, Pelletier explains that the poetic language of the architecture could not be reduced to a single code. By replacing a centuries-old tradition of fixed meaning in architecture with this new, more ambiguous mimetic language, Le Camus granted the user an interpretive – perhaps, a dramaturgical – role in creating spatial stories and ordering experience.

Character theory is not generally thought of as a subversive moment in architectural history. Its more frivolous manifestations lead some socially engaged historians to disregard it altogether. But for Pelletier, the value of *The Genius of Architecture* is dual: Le Camus's architecture conveys meanings both through its form and through what is known as the architectural programme – the intended uses for the building, the events and activities it will host. In her view, this braiding together of architecture with mimesis and affect is the key to ensuring that contemporary architecture does not descend into empty formalism – formal experimentation that has little or no relevance outside the discipline. She looks to her late eighteenth-century case study (politically vexed and paradoxical as it is) not for any hard-and-fast rules about the dramatic organisation of space which, when applied to our current context, would serve only to make buildings reminiscent of a past era, but for ways to restore architecture's commonality and social worth.

Initiating communicative space

Dalibor Vesely also asserts architecture's communicative role. In *Architecture in the Age of Divided Representation* (2004), Vesely reviews assumptions about architecture that have gone (largely) unchallenged for centuries. Turning first to the works of Plato, he argues that our failure to see architecture's basis in mimesis closes down the possibilities for exploring architecture's social usefulness. Vesely rejects what he sees as the 'unfortunate distinction drawn between mimetic and nonmimetic arts' in Plato's writings (p. 367). Plato developed his views (which are expounded most forcefully in book 10 of *The Republic*, *c*.360 BCE) in part as a polemic against the Sophists, a loose collection of itinerant intellectuals whose love of rhetoric and moral relativism are likely to have provoked his harsh judgement of mimetic arts as inferior copies that can mislead viewers. Instead, Vesely concentrates on Aristotle's *Poetics*.

Vesely argues that the broader terms of Aristotle's concept of mimesis can be taken up in architecture, even though Aristotle does not expressly do this. For Aristotle, mimesis is more than simple mimicry or the straightforward visual correspondence between things. In chapter 6 of his *Poetics*, Aristotle overturns Plato's fault-finding evaluation of mimesis and alters its meaning by re-defining it in relation to two other concepts: mythos – the poetic structuring of events – and praxis – a total situation in which human thought has been put into action according to ethical principles. Mimesis, which Aristotle claims achieves its fullest expression in the drama of Greek tragedy, is thus temporalised and spatialised; it is a representation of events that unfold in an environment in which people act and are acted upon. This mimesis–praxis–mythos combination is what makes Aristotle's concept of mimesis more creative and more edifying than Plato's. It is also, through its concern with the material context in which events play out, what enables Vesely to claim that 'architecture, like any other art, is a representation of human praxis' (p. 371). So, architecture can be thought of as a mediating force in the world – one that allows for the expression and interrogation of human thought, action and experience.

What might a mimetic architecture look like in practice? To pick an example from the historical context in which

Aristotle was writing, the architectural principles of ancient Greece included order, proportion, symmetry, harmony, distribution, rhythm and mechanics. Of course, architecture meant buildings. But it also meant articulating the order of the cosmos and contemporary beliefs about the place of people within a social and spiritual totality. We can see this in the 'cosmic' arrangement of the Greek amphitheatre. Here, the dance of the celestial bodies – indeed, the very mathematics and proportions of the universe – is mirrored in the dance of the dancers and in the 'astrological' geometry of the theatre – a circle divided into twelve sections (as in the houses of the zodiac). From this point of view, mimesis is not a simplistic imitation of appearances but a means of embodying human thought – in this case, the prevailing ideology or world-view of ancient Greek culture.

Vesely believes that the recent narrow emphasis on instrumentality and an ever-growing pressure on architects to bow to the demands of capital have brought architecture to a point of crisis. For him, the task we face now is 'how to reconcile the inventions and achievements of modern technology [...] with the conditions of human life, our inherited culture, and the natural world' (p. 7). In his opinion, architectural theorists have been slow to address social and cultural issues on account of the recent tendency to associate architecture with the STEM subjects – science, technology, engineering and mathematics. Architecture's affiliation with hard sciences has left it somewhat out of touch with the critical cultural commentaries that have come out of schools of arts, humanities and social sciences. Vesely argues that in order to see architecture play a meaningful role in society, we must turn to its latent capacity to relate abstract ideas and conceptual structures to the concrete situations of everyday life by means of its representational dimension.

I see exciting possibilities in Vesely's idea that the communicative movement between elements of built space, the space of culture and the natural environment requires architecture to rise above geometric space and develop a more profound understanding of cultural conditions and their interpretation. However, I am wary of his reliance on themes of reconciliation, harmony and unity in projects such as a shared urban garden for Spitalfields, London, which he describes as mitigating a clash between commercial and civic interests by providing – literally and mimetically – a strip of common ground on which people from opposing sides could meet and, eventually, resolve their differences (p. 348). It seems to me that there are some cultural rifts and some repressed aspects of the politico-economic context in which architecture operates that should not be grassed over. Other commentators note the way that mimesis can highlight the tensions that exist between form, programme, site and other aspects of context and can exacerbate ambiguity – or even conflict – in order to prompt critical reflection and to provoke action.

Developing critical representational strategies

Hilde Heynen provides the most explicitly political take on architecture's representational aspect in her book *Architecture and Modernity* (1999). Her argument, which is indebted to the theory of Theodor Adorno, rests on the thought that mimesis involves a kind of doubling by which it is hinted that the 'reality' of the real might have been different, that another way of doing things – an alternate reality – was always possible. The logic underpinning this is that if architecture, through mimesis, can embody the inharmonious aspects of dwelling, creating moments that jar or raise uncomfortable questions, it can develop critical representational strategies.

In his *Aesthetic Theory* (1970), Adorno examines how artworks use mimesis to expose some aspect of reality that would otherwise have remained buried. The reason this is crucial, in Adorno's view, is that we are blinded by a false idea that the world is as it is and cannot be otherwise. Consequently, we fail to see and act upon opportunities for change. Although very little of Adorno's major text on aesthetics concerns architecture, and he wrote only one article that addresses the discipline head on ('Functionalism Today', 1965), his insights into architecture, mimesis and an approach to philosophy called negative dialectics – thinking through contradiction that refuses the consolation of synthesis or the reconciliation of opposites – provide Heynen with the grounds for re-thinking architectural practice as a force for negative critique rather than a mute affirmation of the status quo.

In investigating this possibility, Heynen asks: 'can architecture, by making use of mimesis, consciously and deliberately or otherwise, develop strategies by which it can present itself as *critical* architecture?' (p. 198). This is a hugely problematic question in the context of capitalist societies since private ownership of property would seem to prohibit any such possibility. As she points out, architecture is determined by a variety of social and economic factors: 'not only materials and techniques but also context and programme are the net result of a series of social determinants' (p. 198). However, even in the most compromised of architectural projects, Heynen argues, there is always a moment of artistic autonomy: a moment of pure artistry. This moment provides the opportunity for the architect to fulfil the client's brief but also to signal something else: something that could undercut or even negate the official rhetoric.

It strikes me that something of this sort happens in MY Studio/Höweler + Yoon Architecture's *Low Rez Hi Fi* (2005), a dual-component public art–architecture work designed for a commercial client in Washington, DC, and documented in J. Meejin Yoon's 'Public Works' (2008). The 'low rez' installation uses LED matrices within glass vitrines (one inside the building, running perpendicular to the façade, and another outside) to form an electronic signage display that incorporates images of passersby as they interact with the work. The display screens meet the client's branding needs by creating a high-visibility media and performance piece that draws people's attention from the pavement into the company's foyer. In this way, the 'low rez' part fulfils the client's desire to connect private and public space. And yet the fact that the vitrines are placed either side of a glass boundary could be seen as representing and reinforcing the very ideas of division that the client is seeking to hide or dissolve. Moreover, since the project uses the building's security cameras to capture people's images and shadow them across the screens, it mimics and twists the use of hi-tech security to protect commercial buildings, prompting us to question our growing reliance on media and surveillance mechanisms. In doing this, it raises itself above standard commercial architecture. Its mimetic element introduces a note of criticism into the design.

My second example responds to Heynen's sense that mimesis, through its 'endless resonance', keeps working to prevent simple definition (p. 208). The Museum of Memory and Human Rights in Santiago, Chile, completed in 2009 by Marcos Figueroa of the São Paulo-based practice Estudio America, remembers the tens of thousands of Chileans killed or tortured under the 1973–90 dictatorship of General Augusto Pinochet. It is constructed out of materials native to the land and evocative of traditional industries such as coal mining. These materials act as a reference to common jobs and a shared national heritage. You could say that what is being played out mimetically is a narrative of heroic Chilean endurance and unity, were it not for the fact that the building's skin is covered in broken lines. These jagged lines, cuts or scars suggest a shattered reality: one that cannot be healed by the simple erection of a monument or museum (with all the municipal pride and political vote-scoring that these things too often entail).

This is a spacious and imposing, though unpretentious, building, occupying a whole block to the north-west of the city centre. When you enter, one thing you notice straightaway is a double-height wall covered entirely with photographs of Chile's 'Disappeared'. The effect this wall produces can be taken in meaningfully only from a glass-walled box that protrudes some distance across the exhibition space one storey up from the ground. Standing inside this cube and staring out towards the faces opposite, you get a sudden terrible insight into the experience of loss, since the smiling men, women and children who look back at you can never be reached but only viewed across a void. You want to go up close and look at them properly but you cannot: the architecture deliberately (and brilliantly) disallows it.

Something else is represented in this odd, protruding space as well. Around its perimeter, a number of clear LED-filled cylinders of approximately the same shape and size as the flickering candles inside churches rise up from the floor. The glass cube is, in fact, a *velatón* – a candlelight memorial – apparently offering solace and a place for quiet contemplation. But the fact that the visitor is suspended over a void and is acutely aware of the separation dynamic being played out between cube and wall undermines a wholly comforting reading of this part of the building. What is demonstrated mimetically here – more than ritual tradition and belief – is a sense of the inadequacy of organised religion (or, for that matter, civic or political institutions) to account for such atrocities.

To summarise Heynen's main points: if architecture can harness mimesis, it may find ways to suspend the everyday 'real' and stage moments of subversive intensity. In this way, built space may reveal repressed aspects of building or living, creating ruptures in which we are encouraged to question what we are in danger of forgetting, of blindly accepting or of taking to be self-evident. However, mimesis is not the only theatrically inflected concept to have triggered discussion in architecture in recent years. Next, I consider architecture's growing interest in event-space, performance and the related concept of performativity – notions that stem from the work of Swiss-born architect Bernard Tschumi (1944–).

From event-space to space acts

Spaces and programmes

Bernard Tschumi re-conceived the connections between architectural spaces and actions as a result of his experience of the 1968 student uprisings in Paris and the activities of the Situationist International – a group of intellectuals and artists who, amongst other things, promoted radical alternative approaches to urbanism and movement around cities. His major assertion, as evinced in *The Manhattan Transcripts* (1981), is that architects need to reclaim the architectural programme. In 1994, in the first of three books devoted to the inter-relations between architecture, users and actions, Tschumi declared: 'architecture is as much about the events that take place inside buildings as it is about the buildings themselves' (*Event Cities I*, p. 13). The theatricality of Tschumi's thought comes through in his drawings, with their dramatic shading and strong outlines, and in his preoccupation with themes of violence, murder, eroticism and architecture's unconscious (see the Antonin

Artaud-inspired 'Architecture and Its Double', 1978, and 'Violence of Architecture', 1982). Tschumi's work transforms the way we think of architecture by seeing architecture's end-product – the completed building – as a drama in and of itself and by stressing how architectural *processes*, which begin at concept stage and continue indefinitely as users interact with buildings, are analogous to performance processes, since both are time-based and dynamic.

Throughout his work, but especially in the projects and essays of the 1980s, Tschumi argues that architectural programmes and typologies – abstract building types, such as factories, mosques, office blocks, theatres – have arrived at a point of radical disjunction: buildings designed for particular purposes have been adapted for other uses. This observation casts doubt on the supposed inevitability of the form–function relationship – the mainstay of architectural modernism. It also highlights the fact that architecture cannot absolutely determine how we behave within it. In contrast to the idea that architecture disciplines us and dictates strict spatial and social cues, Tschumi points out that spaces and events have a more complex relationship than we have acknowledged and that architecture–user relations can be renegotiated in unexpected ways. After all, we may designate certain spaces for specific activities – say, kitchens as places for preparing food, or bedrooms as intimate places – but people have sex in their kitchens and eat pizza in bed.

For Tschumi, the disjunction between building types and programmes (and the consequent transformation of the spatial conditions in which we live and act) destabilises normative practices – ways of designing, building, living, behaving that we unthinkingly take to be normal and to exclude all other ways. Conceptualising a politics of architecture and urbanism, Tschumi advocates re-combinations of programme, space and cultural narrative based around three basic tactics: crossprogramming, disprogramming and transprogramming, each of which deliberately disrupts established set-ups in architecture and society to show that other ways of being and doing are possible (*Event Cities I*). For example, Tschumi might 'crossprogramme' the workings of a library inside the spatial configuration of a prison, or make a sports centre out of a car park. Equally, he might 'transprogramme' two very different kinds of event-space – such as a planetarium and a roller coaster – regardless of their incompatibilities. Then again, he might 'disprogramme' a variety of different sets of events and spatial requirements, as in his 1990 competition entry for the Kyoto Railway Station in Japan, where image theatre meets sky lounge, wedding chapel, athletic club, amusement arcade, gourmet market and historical museum, creating a hybrid megaproject. Tschumi's cultural reference for crossprogramming, the first and, in many ways, the most useful of these three (in that it allows for 'sustainable' adaptive re-use of existing buildings), is crossdressing, and its importance lies in its questioning of appearances, categories and customary practices.

Tschumi's ideas, many of which are played out in the ambiguous forms and spatial relationships of his Parc de la Villette, Paris (1998, designed in conversation with the

French philosopher Jacques Derrida), can be helpfully compared to those of thinkers in the fields of language, gender theory and performance studies. All are interested in the braided concepts of performance and performativity; all focus their attention on the ways in which words, bodies and performances come to *mean* and *do* what they do (and on how these meanings and actions might be subverted). And since the theories of all feed into architecture theory now, they deserve a brief exposition.

What is performativity?

The term 'performative' first arose in the context of the philosophy of language, where it was coined by British philosopher John Langshaw Austin to describe a particular kind of speech act: an utterance that *does* something rather than merely describes something in the world (*How to Do Things with Words*, 1962). Examples are:

> 'I declare war' (if, indeed, you have the power to do so, and the circumstances are ripe for war)
>
> 'I do' (as in 'take this woman to be my lawful, wedded wife')
>
> 'I name this ship the *Queen Elizabeth II*' (as uttered by someone in authority when smashing a bottle against its side)

From Austin we learn that, in uttering a performative, you are performing an action, or perhaps performing the primary action in a series of other (non-verbal) actions that have real consequences in the world. Language can bestow forgiveness, blessings, freedom, citizenship and injuries. In other words, language can perform a reality; speech *acts*.

When American philosopher Judith Butler takes up this idea in the context of gender and identity, she defines performativity (using Derrida's 1988 'correction', in 'Signature, Event, Context', to Austin's theory) as a stylised repetition of acts which reiterate and reinforce a set of norms. In *Gender Trouble: Feminism and the Subversion of Identity* (1990), Butler posits gender as a social performance rather than the expression of a prior reality. What she is saying is that neither our gender nor our sexuality stems from some innate property of our being either male or female. Rather, 'normal' gender characteristics accrue over time as we repeat until they become naturalised culturally coded behaviours and internalise them to produce our gender. Performativity, here, is the process of repeating those gestures, habits, dress codes and embodied acts that signal our gender, while performance describes the particular manifestations of this process.

The tensions between performativity and social and theatrical performance are especially acute in drag shows, where men or women crossdress to confuse the 'straight' correlation of anatomical sex with gender. These subversive performances highlight how social norms are forged in the process of performativity and make it is easier for us to imagine alternative performativities. Butler's sense of drag as being at odds with cultural dominants and stable identities is liberating, and it throws further light on Tschumi's notion of crossprogramming as a way to resist certain 'normalising' cultural and architectural pressures that can start to determine the way users think and behave in space. In a moment, we shall see that the active and transgressive connotations of performativity and performance have exciting implications for critical architecture today. First, we should note that performative architecture is not a homogeneous thing and that its manifestations and its politics pull in different directions.

Performative architectures

As a multi-billion-dollar global industry that uses sophisticated technologies (some of which are available only to itself and the militaries of select nation-states), architecture is caught up in both the organisational and the technological challenges to perform that Jon McKenzie describes in his book *Perform or Else* (2001). In business and organisation, performance has to do with maximising productivity, and McKenzie identifies the challenge of performance in this sphere as efficiency. In the area of technology, he explains that when we ask how fast the latest laptop computer is or enquire about its battery life or memory, what we really want to know is: How will it perform? The challenge of technological performance, then, is one of effectiveness. In architecture, the term 'performative' is frequently used as shorthand to describe design practices that meet the combined challenges of efficiency and effectiveness, although it also refers to architecture that is animated by media and electronics and to the performance(s) of intelligent architecture – architecture that uses evolving technology to move and respond to human or environmental stimuli.

Hi-tech strands of performative architecture use digital technologies of quantitative and qualitative performance-based simulation – analytical computational techniques that allow specific design propositions to be evaluated – to redefine expectations of building design. This enables architects to select a solution that offers optimal performance not only in terms of environmental and/or cost-efficiency and technical (structural, thermal, acoustic) effectiveness but also in social and cultural terms: to make buildings that promote new, improved relationships between architecture and user. Chris Salter, in his 2010 book *Entangled: Technology and the Transformation of Performance*, argues that the kinetic and responsive architectures most closely associated with architectural performativity pose complex questions about architecture: Is it still, or can it move? Does it remain the same, or can it shape-shift into new configurations? Is it always permanent, or can it be as fleeting as performance? In theory, this is riveting stuff. In practice, as Salter points out, there is an 'underlying friction between an architecture of performative space and an architecture of performance originating at the level of the intelligent surface' (p. 106). To put it more straightforwardly, too many of the blinking screens and smart surfaces that we are seeing in contemporary performative architecture are simply sensational replacements for conventional materials and do not substantially alter our experience of space.

Countering the tendency towards excessive technological performativity, Branko Kolarevic argues that the role of architects and engineers is 'less to predict, pre-programme or represent the building's performances, than it is to instigate, embed, diversify and multiply their effects' so as to better support 'indeterminate patterns and dynamics of use, and poetics of spatial and temporal change' ('Towards the Performative in Architecture', 2005, p. 212). While Kolarevic's thought reflects a turn to the end-users of buildings, architect Ali Rahim, writing in the same collection, troubles top-down, standardising practices. In calling for architects to 'avoid conventional norms of expression and prescribed interpretation', Rahim echoes Butler and shows how performative architecture, like queer practices of gender construction, can de-essentialise disciplinary norms and create new architectural performativities ('Performativity: Beyond Efficiency and Optimisation in Architecture', 2005, p. 180).

One of the ways in which these performativities are manifesting is through performance architecture – so called to acknowledge its debt to performance art and distinguish it from the more gimmicky hi-tech performative architectures. Performance architecture explores the possibilities for 'architect-performed buildings' – where the architect becomes a kind of performance artist – and for design that responds to the human body and interaction, where the everyday rituals of people living in, working in or passing through a space are used to generate the architecture. Experiments such as Alex Schweder and Ward Shelly's *Stability* (Lawrimore

Project, Seattle, 2009), where a tiny apartment suspended from the ceiling see-sawed whenever one of its occupants moved to one end, Didier Fiuza Faustino's *Double Happiness* (Shenzhen–Hong Kong Bi-City Biennale of Urbanism and Architecture, 2009), which transformed an advertising bill-board into a pair of high-rise city swings, and the *Performing Architecture* events (Tate Britain, London, 2013), in which Schweder and Lamis Bayer devised a series of playful instructions and inscribed them on the walls of the Duveen Galleries, are invitations to users to change spaces and struc-tures by enacting them differently. Most of these projects are playful, and although some are too tightly 'scripted' to allow for full and genuinely democratic user participation, many merge event-space, sociality and play with a politics of archi-tecture and performance. I conclude this part of the book by looking at a project in performance-led theatre architecture which exemplifies how performance and performativity can trouble cherished industry orthodoxies and empower users of architecture. The project is called Playgrounds and the architect is Haworth Tompkins.

Theatre architecture as scratch performance

Battersea Arts Centre (BAC) in south-west London occu-pies Battersea's former town hall, an 1893 building designed for civic function and ceremony by the architect E. W. Mountford. It was re-tooled as a community arts venue hosting three studio theatres in 1980. From its inaugura-tion until the early years of this century, the centre pro-grammed its black box studios, leaving most of the rest of its seventy-four-room building poorly used. By 2006, BAC's Grade 2* listed building was badly in need of technical upgrades and repair, and Haworth Tompkins was hired to carry out the works. The fact that BAC would have to remain open throughout the redevelopment provided the immediate impetus for a series of phased interventions in which changes were made in response to performers' needs and could fade in or out of focus depending on how busy the venue was at any moment.

In formulating a tactical working method, Haworth Tompkins looked to BAC's scratch performance techniques, where performance pieces are shown at various stages of their development to an outside audience, whose feedback guides the further development of the work. Translated into an architectural method, scratch results in a provisional and radically inclusive approach which breaks with established modes of practice. In place of the mainstream architectural scenario, in which a team of very expensive experts rolls out a solution, often to the bewilderment of a building's occupants, Haworth Tompkins's work at BAC involves the arts organisation and its users in an iterative architectural process in which each testing-of-an-idea-through-doing-it provides opportunities to improve on previous iterations. Architect Steve Tompkins's description of the process reveals clear similarities between his architecture and the work of practice-based researchers in performance:

> If you allow yourself to enter into the conversation, where you're just going along, talking,

suggesting, scribbling, pinning things up on the wall, ripping them down again – and it's just that constant level of contact – often ideas will just come through osmosis, through leaps, and authorship is blurred. (Steve Tompkins, interviewed by Robert John Brocklehurst and Juliet Rufford for 'Scratching BAC', 2011)

And, like a practice-based research cycle in performance, Haworth Tompkins's work at BAC has yielded three important insights.

First, it has shown how a building never has a steady state but is active and unstable, visibly shifting, growing, and shedding and gathering layers in time to the rhythms of its occupants. During the first phase of works at BAC, Haworth Tompkins adopted ideas about creating sneak routes around the building that Punchdrunk performance collective conceived while devising *The Masque of the Red Death* (2007–8). The architects revealed hidden doors and broke through partition walls, leaving these changes in place afterwards. Other alterations, including lowered ceilings and partition walls, have been retained and, over time, may become indistinguishable from the permanent architecture of BAC. Tompkins explains the improvisatory, cumulative nature of the work:

We make small interventions, feeding into specific performances and these will leave a trace, an accretion which will gradually accumulate.

> And, eventually, like a coral reef perhaps, the
> building will transform into a different space, a
> different environment ... but over evolutionary
> periods of time. So, even though each interven-
> tion might be a day, or a week, or six months,
> the time period of the project is ... twenty years,
> say? ... Or more? (Tompkins interview)

While each new articulation of the space is actively shaping
the performance work being done in, on and through it,
subsequent seasons of theatre will inscribe themselves onto
the long-term character of the space. The active, unpre-
dictable nature of the interaction encourages theatre and
architecture to engage each other in an on-going process of
creative re-definition.

The second insight bears out Tschumi's claims about
the redundancy of fixed typology–programme relationships. At the same time as Haworth Tompkins was helping
Punchdrunk make adjustments and additions to enhance
the space, it was also returning the arts centre to a more
explicitly 'found' state. Whereas the 1980 conversion of
the building tried to expunge all trace of Victorian town
hall, Haworth Tompkins's work has aimed at rediscovering
the complexity and ambiguity that occurred when the arts
organisation first moved in and started using a building not
designed for theatre. Tompkins's claim that 'people understand what a building like this is about, and they accept the
invitation of the building just to go and explore, get lost
in it' underscores Tschumi's point about disjunction by

suggesting that mismatches between building type and use – rather than a strict alignment of form and function – may be beneficial to theatre precisely on account of the friction they create (Tompkins interview). This might sound obvious to theatre folks; it is not always clear to some architects.

Once the legitimacy of the converted studio spaces had been problematised, it became easier to see the theatrical potential of other areas of the building. At first-floor level, Haworth Tompkins unveiled a sequence of inter-connected domestic-scale rooms, which Punchdrunk director Felix Barrett used as intimate performance environments before gathering the audience for a finale inside the 800-seat Grand Hall. Both architecture and theatre production broke free from the confines of the traditional auditorium, tearing down the boundaries that separate acting space from audience space, front- from back-of-house. This experiment in crossprogramming a town hall and a theatre enables a wider variety of performer–spectator relationships than can be found in most conventional auditoria. By installing a building-wide plug-and-play system which makes technical hardware available on demand in designated and non-designated performance spaces, the architects have been able to retain the layout and language of the town hall while enabling practitioners to find, or create, exactly the right spatial context for their work.

Third, BAC Playgrounds brings to light possibilities for a flexible approach to the architectural programme of works. Because the building had to stay open, the architects needed to re-think how architects do architecture and why they do it in the way they do. Haworth Tompkins discovered that building works can be programmed in the same way as you might programme a schedule of rehearsals, workshops or performances. It invented what it calls 'the space programme', where architectural interventions are timetabled so that if, say, there is a rehearsal going on in BAC's Council Chamber at eleven o'clock, then at half past one the architects might do some work before the space is needed later in the afternoon for a youth theatre workshop. Architecture is thus one of the daily activities of the arts centre and is no longer bracketed as distinct from the performance work that goes on inside it. This has major implications for building design as it brings architects and clients into closer and (potentially) more collaborative contact, allowing architects to gain an understanding of working practices in a dissimilar field and to make changes in response to felt needs.

Architecture's manipulation by Haworth Tompkins is being undertaken with full consciousness of what the practice is rejecting or transforming in architectural terms: excessive functionalism certainly, and any idea about theatre as a fixed typology, but also the notion that architecture is something that can be done only by architects. In acknowledging the rigidity with which architecture has operated in our recent history, and exploring the performative potential of these minimal, on-going moves, Haworth Tompkins is challenging industry norms, ideas about authorship in architecture and the behavioural codes of theatre as they are promoted through architecture's tendency to channel and contain us. Similarly, it strikes me that Haworth Tompkins's use of performance techniques to 'devise' architectural solutions and de-essentialise accepted ways of doing things might help architecture reinvent itself not as an exercise in rational space-planning but, through its 'space acts', as a practice that re-thinks what architecture *is* by concentrating on what it *does* and what it might *enable*.

part two: on theatre

Theatre, architecture and illusion
Illusion's framework

Theatre involves pretend. Sometimes, this leads to conventions of staging and play-acting that are, frankly, pretentious. (Both Copeau and his compatriot Artaud hated the overblown acting styles and social one-upmanship of turn-of-the-twentieth-century theatre in France.) At other times, it involves magic, tricks-of-the-eye and spectacular delights that are admired precisely because they are illusions. Often, the invitation to pretend is partial and paradoxical. We see this in theatre traditions where believable elements (psychologically convincing characters, for example) are combined with the patently untrue (supernatural and fantastical elements) or with aspects of metadrama or metatheatre (when the play-text or production steps 'outside' itself to comment on what is happening). Occasionally, the pull to pretend is very strong and we are led to believe in what we see so completely that we do not question it but are seduced into accepting its fictions. This occurs whenever the mimetic likeness is all-consuming and spectators lose sight of the mimetic gap – the breach between seeming and being. In all, dramatic illusionism has enjoyed such a hold on the European imagination and on theatre cultures informed by the European tradition that its various manifestations have dominated the art-form since the Renaissance.

Tied to the ways in which dramatic illusionism produces its effects on audiences is the move, throughout the late sixteenth and early seventeenth centuries, from outdoor theatre to the indoor playhouse. The conscious emergence of the art of theatre architecture in Europe at this time had far-reaching consequences for modern theatre traditions because the way we see and understand staged events depends, to a great extent, on how they are framed and presented. If theatre architecture creates the conditions in which we interpret what we see, we will need to consider the role it plays in organising action and shaping reception if we are to make sense of the theatre event. But how exactly does theatre architecture direct our view and influence our understanding? And what are the politics of such a construct?

The stage type most commonly associated with illusionistic theatre – the proscenium-arch stage – developed around the taste for perspectival staging, or the playing of scenes against an illusion of deep space created through the use of artificial perspective (for a more detailed explanation of perspective drawing and its use in the theatre see Dominic Johnson, *Theatre & the Visual*, 2012, pp. 23–31). The 1545 publication of Serlio's designs for temporary stages to be constructed from timber scaffolding inside the great halls of ducal palaces in Renaissance Italy was highly influential. Serlio's idea was for an inclined stage which would slope upwards and away from the audience and on which receding sets of grooves would hold in place scenic items built and painted in perspective. With this innovation, audiences could be shown a framed illusion of life beyond the palace walls. But artistic developments such as this are rarely devoid of ideological implications. Christine Boyer, in *The City of Collective Memory* (1996), explains how the framed pictorial view offers a unified composition or homogeneous world-view which excludes extraneous elements and hides peripheral subthemes from sight, thus 'reflect[ing] the presence of an all-seeing and all-knowing authority controlling the scene' (p. 81). The stunning perspectival effects, which were measured from a central vanishing point behind the scene and were fully revealed only to the princely seat positioned directly opposite, set up a relationship between theatrical illusion, architecture, eye-point and authority. Theatre architecture not only forms and manipulates audiences' perspectives on events but also upholds social hierarchies and ideologically laden visions of the world.

In post-revolutionary France, the new bourgeoisie did away with spectacles of sovereign power and staged realistic tableaux of middle-class life and morality in their place. Perspectival illusions in two dimensions gave way to realism and the use of three-dimensional box sets viewed through the proscenium opening, or 'fourth wall'. But realism is also an illusion. Indeed, as several of the authors in Joe Kelleher and Nicholas Ridout's edited collection *Contemporary Theatres in Europe* (2006) also argue, the more real what we seem to see on-stage is, the more illusionistic paraphernalia it needs to support it.

From the 1870s to the end of the century, in a bid to make plays look as life-like as possible, practitioners opted for verisimilitude – extreme truth to life. Exponents of naturalism approximated the architectural 'real' as an authenticating device, using a densely furnished stage world and clever suggestions of other rooms extending off-stage to persuade audiences that they were peering into the actual living room of Torvald and Nora's *petit-bourgeois* townhouse in Henrik Ibsen's *A Doll's House* (1879), or into the very kitchen in which the wayward heroine of August Strindberg's *Miss Julie* (1888) would seal her fate with her father's servant, Jean. The detail was beguiling. But no sooner had naturalism reached the heights of believability than a disparate group of experimenters sought to bring it down. They did this by turning architecture against itself. What was at stake for them in doing this? And how could architecture, which was complicit in creating the realist–naturalist illusion, be used to dismantle the very framework it had helped to establish?

The shock of the architectural real

The backlash against illusionism by members of the historical avant-gardes was fundamentally caught up with the advent of twentieth-century modernity and motivated by a mixture of ideological, spatial and politico-economic concerns: from the shift to mass production to the 'scientific' organisation of work in factories, and from radical changes to the way people experienced time, space and communication (e.g. through the cinema and the telephone) to mechanised warfare and the mass, technologised killing of World War I. For practitioners as different from one another as Adolphe Appia, Artaud, Bertolt Brecht, Edward Gordon Craig, Filippo Tommaso Marinetti, Vsevolod Meyerhold, László Moholy-Nagy, Oskar Schlemmer and Tristan Tzara, the mechanisms by which the audience of fourth-wall theatre is persuaded to believe that the dramatic world is real, including the design strategies used in building believable stage space, resulted in theatre that was (in Craig's opinion) false and hypocritical (*Towards a New Theatre*, 1913, p. 6). Breaking the ties that bound illusionistic theatre to bourgeois norms and the fixed eye-point of authority, theatre-makers of the historical avant-gardes rejected centred, perspectival representations of life as propagandist. In a range of ways, these practitioners challenged the model of the bifurcated proscenium-arch auditorium as the classic means of upholding the division between art and life (through the detached view) and turned their attention, instead, to layered perspectives, multiple viewpoints and the modern restructuring of social relations during an aggressive phase of capitalist expansion.

To oppose the realist illusion, some theatre-makers sought a wholly different form of performance space. Louis Jouvet worked on Copeau's 'architectural' stage – a form that incorporated different levels and distinct playing areas but was stripped of all décor so that it could only ever be perceived as a stage and not as a representation of some other place. Appia, rejecting perspectival staging for the way its two-dimensional, 'pictorial' logic contradicts the three-dimensionality of the (real) actor's body, championed the new atelier or studio theatre, where he could treat stage space as a cubic volume and not a flat picture plane. Meanwhile, Artaud sought out some lowly hangar or barn from which to defy the theatre establishment and wring out the question of theatre's purpose and place in society. A few, such as Bauhaus founder-director Walter Gropius and Austrian-American architect Frederick Kiesler, worked on bold designs for theatre architecture which might speak to the complex and chaotic systems of mechanisation and industrial mass production conditioning the modern experience. Both Kiesler's Endless Theatre (1924) and Gropius's Total Theater (1927) drew on scientific theories to shatter the kind of socio-spatial homogeneity espoused by the princely and bourgeois theatres. These experiments showed that it is possible to re-think the architectural type and, in so doing, to investigate the conditions under which theatre operates.

Others remained within the traditional proscenium-arch theatre but highlighted its spatial codes in a self-reflexive investigation of theatrical possibility and the conditions of spectatorship. For example, Marinetti's Futurist manifesto 'The Variety Theatre' (1913) presupposes a traditional Italianate auditorium but calls for its violent disruption through action that develops simultaneously on the stage, in the boxes and in the orchestra. By splitting apart position-alities and points of view inside the theatre, Marinetti fore-grounded structures of production, perception and social organisation. Thus, he replaced the authority of the singular (princely) view and showed that viewpoints and positions are neither natural nor politically neutral.

Another provocative tactic was to deploy functional architectonic elements (e.g. staircases, bridges, ramps and columns) in place of the expected scenery. Since the archi-tectural object belongs to the real world, and is not part of a perspectival or box set illusion, its presence on the stage is anomalous if not 'shocking' to audiences. The Russian Constructivists exploited architecture's associations with organisation and production to model new strategies for social and political (re)construction. The strength of this approach is the role it gives audiences both in the produc-tion of artistic meaning and in imagining social and politi-cal possibilities not yet constituted. If, according to the Constructivists, theatre is not passive but is an active part of production (in its broadest sense of a society-building and culture-forming labour), architecture as the art of imagin-ing and building new forms can aid theatre in realising its active, organisational role.

By the early 1930s, architecture had transformed mod-ern staging practices, providing the theatre with a powerful means to challenge realism's hegemony, distinguish itself from the pictorial arts as embodied, three-dimensional experience, convey possibilities for organisation and pro-duction in theatre and everyday life, trouble traditional perspectives on performance and spatial designations such as 'stage' and 'auditorium' (and who belongs in each of these), and imagine what complex new relationships might exist between bodies, objects, spaces and machines at a time of rapid political, economic, scientific and philosophical change. Whether as dynamic object on the stage or as dynamic space enabling different interactions and experiences, architecture provided a valuable means to challenge the ideologies of illusionist theatre's aesthetics.

Architecturally speaking, the theatre of the historical avant-gardes is a hard act to follow. And yet experimenting with architectural forms, processes and associations in performance is still replete with meaning. If, for avant-garde practitioners, architecture's perceived 'real thing-ness' provided ways to counter illusionism and destabilise narratives of authority and homogeneity, some theatre-makers working within the media-saturated societies, spectatorial cities and service economies of late capital are finding that architecture's ambiguous position within contemporary culture, as much as its complex mixture of tradition and hi-tech, gives it a peculiar purchase on the forces – political, economic, ecological, technological, corporate and social – that shape and constrain our lives. In the altered circumstances of the present, where the illusions to which we are prey are those of 'immaterial' or 'affective' labour (discussed in more detail below), the efficient circulation of capital through international banking systems and money markets, the dream of private property ownership (with its concomitant idealisation and defence of domestic space) and escape into a virtual existence where contacts, lifestyles and identities can be taken up and discarded at will, architectural traits, techniques and technologies are proving helpful to theatre that questions the way we live and work now.

Next, I look at two ways in which I think architecture helps theatre practitioners to grapple with some contemporary illusions. First, I consider how recent pieces of theatre and dance-performance have used architectural fragments and acts of building and un-building to explore their own 'produced-ness' and to raise broader questions about the nature of labour and production. Then, I suggest how theatre and architecture, as practices based on a central image of the house, offer critical traction to performers currently engaging questions of shelter and dwelling.

Labour, production and im/materiality

In the advanced economies, in the mutation of industrial to post-industrial capital that has taken place since the 1960s, questions about work and production have become hard to pin down. 'All that is solid has', as Karl Marx so rightly predicted, 'melted into air' (*Communist Manifesto*, 1848, p. 223). The service economies of global capitalism thrive on immaterial labour – labour that produces an immaterial or 'affective' product (e.g. customer care provided through call centres or hospitality provided by travel reps). These intangible, traceless products are aimed at increasing our feelings of ease, well-being or excitement while disguising the work that goes into producing them. But, as political theorists Michael Hardt and Antonio Negri stress, 'immaterial labour almost always mixes with material forms of labour: health care workers, for example, perform affective, cognitive and linguistic tasks together with material ones, such as cleaning bedpans and changing bandages' (*Multitude: War and Democracy in the Age of Empire*, 2004, p. 109). Performance is implicated in this process in ways that many of us might find uncomfortable. Performance trains managerial subjects – public or private sector workers whose identities and subjectivities are caught up within systems of managerial control – to respond to cues from others and switch quickly between a large number of different roles. At best, it teaches confidence, flexibility, teamwork and a capacity to improvise; at worst, it encourages people to be inauthentic, to put on a good show, to sustain the 'magic' whatever it takes. If performance is a key skillset in the sphere of immaterial labour and production, a resistant theatre practice will want to highlight and counter this situation. But how might it do so?

In her essay 'Tech Support: Labour in the Global Theatres of The Builders Association and Rimini Protokoll' (2011), performance theorist Shannon Jackson claims that the challenge for theatre-makers now is 'to find in the exposure of material and immaterial registers in contemporary (capitalist) culture evidence of their intimate and ever-shifting co-imbrication' (p. 149). She reasons that theatre, having always straddled the material and the immaterial, is ideally placed to respond to this imperative (p. 146). I agree that theatre has this advantage, although one (possible) problem is that audiences will be too habituated to the curious, and generally benign, way theatrical performance uses (material) bodies in making its immaterial product for the critique to hit its mark. This is where architecture comes in. Jackson notes how companies such as The Builders Association and Rimini Protokoll borrow techniques from architecture, as well as from installation, sculpture and video, to 'expand or redistribute the effects of theatrical engagement [...] by incorporating those technologies into the medium of enactment or by offering counter-spaces that anachronistically – and hence provocatively – return us to the low-tech space of personal encounter' (pp. 144–45). Enmeshed within the economic and technological forces of globalisation, and yet figuring as an emphatically material provocation on the stage, architecture can help theatre unveil the performative 'illusion' of the immaterial sphere and reveal the materials, tools and hard graft needed to construct it. The 1989 dance-theatre piece *Palermo Palermo* by Pina Bausch's Tanztheater Wuppertal might serve as an example.

Critical discussion about *Palermo Palermo*, which forms part of Bausch's travelogue series of dances about cities, is usually couched in terms of urban fragmentation and urban detritus caused as much by societal codes and cultural events as by the earthquakes that rock the whole of Sicily. The piece is framed by acts of structural failure and landscape design: at the start, in one of the most audacious openings in theatre, five tonnes of rubble from a full-height breezeblock wall, erected across the proscenium line, is collapsed onto the stage; at the end, a stage crew comes on to 'plant' blossom trees for a projected final scene. Certainly, productions of this work, including the one I saw at London's Sadler's Wells in 2012, reveal a deep unease about the stability of those things we have built to protect us: not only walls and houses but also the entire set-up of Mafia-riddled, Roman Catholic southern Italian society. They also suggest that out of decay there may come a chance to re-build – indeed, earthquake zones provide the prime opportunity for young architects to innovate, since many of the formal restrictions on planning and construction are temporarily suspended in these crisis space-times. But there is something else going on here, too.

The something else that I think is demonstrated in *Palermo Palermo* is the staging of labour. The piles of breeze-blocks littering the stage of Sadler's Wells placed extraordinary demands on the dancers, who had to pick their way across them on tottering stiletto heels or else in bare feet. At the same time as alluding to the ruins of Europe, the fall of the Berlin Wall and, with it, the Soviet bloc, these architectural fragments testified to the blood-and-sweat skill involved in making an ethereal production – dance – look effortless. By extension, the piece showed the embodied, task-based nature of all performance. It also provided the occasion, towards the end of the first half, for the stage hands to come on and start removing the breezeblocks – a job that cut through the false separation of immaterial product and material process, mixing on-stage and back-stage worlds in a chain-dance of choreographed gestures, and linking theatrical aesthetics to the logistics of putting on a show. Both theatre and architecture are productions. One reason *Palermo Palermo* is significant is that it stages a related set of concerns around collective labour and artistic and social inter-dependence in ways that belie capitalism's – and illusionist theatre's – tendency to gloss over the realities and conditions of production. Offset against one another, the architectural and ephemeral elements of the piece show how the material is already hidden within the immaterial, and open up possibilities for uncovering similar inter-dependencies between the immaterial and the material, labour and production in the world beyond the theatre.

Jackson's piece, which has influenced my own analysis of the themes of labour, production and im/materiality, is primarily about 'new media theatre' critiques of globalisation and the digitally connected supply chains of the call centre industry, but it references several productions by The Builders Association that are more architecturally oriented and that reveal a concern with material (as well as immaterial or affective) labour. Indeed, Jackson includes a brief analysis of The Builders Association's first-ever show, a reworking of Ibsen's *The Master Builder* (1892) called simply *Master Builder* (1994), as evidence of the company's long-standing interest in the theme of labour. The most prominent feature of this production was its architectural set: a three-storey house prized open along its vertical axis and standing inside the 17,000-square-foot industrial warehouse which the company was using as a temporary venue. The split house was inspired by artist Gordon Matta-Clark's 'anarchitectural' interventions into real buildings – radical deconstructions, including *Splitting* (Englewood, NJ, USA, 1974) and *Conical Intersect* (Paris, 1975), that hover nervously between stability and precariousness. The act of building and then dismantling a house in *Master Builder* provided a means to express Ibsen's themes of cloud-castles, doomed projects, loss and the longing for meaningful work while mounting a self-reflexive enquiry into The Builders Association's own work. Company architect John Cleater designed the set in conversation with director Marianne Weems to re-frame the 1892 drama of architectural ambition as, in part, an investigation into the company's labour of building – an activity Jackson understands as continuing to animate its interventions into mediascapes where manual work and construction seem oddly outmoded activities (p. 151).

Among the particular strengths of Jackson's analysis of *Master Builder* is its sense that building and craft might act as 'provocative anachronisms', counterbalancing the ephemerality of performance and some of the uses to which performance is put in our global economies of labour (p. 145). The 'intrusion' of master carpenter Joel Cichowski, in a pre-show demonstration of the tools he had used in constructing the set, reminds us that even the most immaterial form of labour still requires real human bodies engaged in concrete tasks in actual, physical space. And yet the split house of the production was not quite the primitive hut it might, at first, have seemed. Wired with MIDI triggers that the performers activated to set off sound effects, music and video, it was also a performative architecture, mixing the material and the technological to produce its immaterial effects. What *Master Builder* showed – and what subsequent productions by The Builders Association in collaboration with architects Diller + Scofidio (*Jet Lag*, 1998) and with commercial design company dbox (*Supervision*, 2005) have further elaborated – is that the paradoxes of architecture provide performance with an appropriately ambiguous set of circumstances, tools, materials and affects with which to question the enigmas of labour, production and im/materiality. In addition to the dialectic between the 'old' craft of building and today's new media technologies, then, the company explores architecture's status as contradictory confluence of art and commerce, fantasy and pragmatism, virtual technology and manual labour as a key (of sorts) to understanding that potent blend of seeming opposites in today's late capitalist societies.

Dreams of house and home

Although popular housing is not normally thought of as architecture proper, a recurring theme in architectural discourse from ancient times to the present day identifies the house as the origin and archetype of architecture. Theatre has also been thought of as a house. Marvin Carlson's entry for an alphabet of theatrical terms, 'H for House' (2013), traces the historical usage of the word 'house' (a contraction of the early modern 'playhouse') to refer to the theatre buildings of Restoration England, and from shortly after that time to refer to both the audience and auditorium of European and American theatres. So firm had the association between the theatrical and the residential house become by the late nineteenth century that parts of the interiors of one began to resemble those of the other. Indeed, as Hugh Maguire claims, the theatre of Victorian England provided middle-class audiences not merely with a 'house' but with a veritable 'home from home' as theatre architects responded to softer, more personal tastes in décor and furnishing ('Victorian Theatre as Home from Home', 2000). While the past hundred years have seen a decline in use of the term 'house' to describe either auditorium or entire theatre building, there may now be grounds for reclaiming the idea of the theatre as a house.

To push a point made by Jonathan Hill in *Immaterial Architecture* (2006), the ideal of the house as home, as a refuge full of objects and memories, has never been more widely desired – and harder to achieve – than at this time of uneven development, precarious employment and rising property prices (p. 26). More than 50 per cent of the world's population now lives in cities, and the construction industry represents anywhere from 6 to 18 per cent of GDP on average in Europe. Yet whole streets of residential housing in parts of northern England and in American cities such as Baltimore and Detroit are boarded up. In these circumstances, architecture becomes part of a highly charged and contested problematic, and artists who respond to the accelerated pace of urban development and to housing crises worldwide frequently find themselves working at the interstices of theatre and architecture – performatively critiquing patterns of ownership and dispossession.

Some theatre-makers explore these issues on the stage, using architecture in a way that reprises the shock tactics of the historical avant-gardes while re-tooling them for the current context. In 2011, The Builders Association's *House/Divided* (Wexner Centre, Columbus, Ohio) projected financial data relating to the US housing crash onto a set made of fabric from a (real) foreclosed house. The mixed-media piece used John Steinbeck's Depression-era novel *The Grapes of Wrath* (which chronicles the eviction and displacement of the Joad family) to question the robustness of house and home as structure, idea and lived reality now. In another example, Javanese experimental theatre group Teater Garasi used a 'junk' architecture of carpet rolls and corrugated tin to record the plight of Jakarta's five-million-plus slum-dwellers for a piece called *Je.ja.l.an* (*The Crowded Streets*, Taman Budaya, Yogyakarta, 2008). In its depiction of people improvising makeshift shacks (as they are forced to along the banks of the Ciliwung river), Teater Garasi underscored the fact that architecture is a developed-world commodity needed desperately elsewhere.

Other artists have tackled housing crisis, displacement and homelessness in the streets and cities where it is happening. Krzysztof Wodiczko's 1988 intervention *The Homeless Vehicle Project* (New York City) remains exemplary. Wodiczko designed a number of trolley-cum-sleeping-pods for use by homeless men. The point was both practical and political. The vehicles were multi-functional but they were also very eye-catching. This ensured that the men, and the homelessness affecting them, could not be hidden away as civic chauvinism's dirty secret but would receive the public attention they deserved. Thus, in Rosalyn Deutsche's words, Wodiczko '"dramatise[d]" the operations of a politico-economic system built on hiding the problem of homelessness while refusing to use public funds to finance the substantive construction of decent permanent housing' (*Evictions*, 1996, p. 97). Chilean artist Alfredo Jaar's activist artwork on behalf of homeless Québécois, *Lights in the City* (Montréal, 1999), also aimed to make homelessness visible. Jaar installed 100,000 watts of red light inside the cupola – small dome – on top of the Marché Bonsecours, a landmark monument in the old port area of the city, and rigged three nearby homeless shelters with 'detonating devices'. Every time someone entered a shelter, they could push a button to illuminate the cupola with a flash of red light – an immaterial architecture that sent their 'distress call' out across the city. In these examples, architecture provides artists and performers with a visible, tangible means to make socially engaged work.

Still more have found that the use of residential homes charges art and performance work about home with an urgency that would be less easy to achieve elsewhere. Rachel Whiteread studies themes of domestic space, dwelling and loss in sculpture and photography made in relation to abandoned or condemned homes (e.g. *Ghost*, Chisenhale Gallery, London, 1990; *House*, 193 Grove Road, London, 1993; *Demolished*, Tate Modern, London, 1993–95). Meanwhile, Matthias Lilienthal's project *X Wohnungen* (*X Homes*, 2003–13) took audiences into apartments in the poorer suburbs of Duisburg, Berlin, Caracas, Vienna, São Paulo, Johannesburg, Warsaw, Istanbul, Mannheim and

Beirut for a series of intimate performances and art installations which challenged perceptions about local immigrant groups, long-term residents and housing districts that are decidedly off theatre's beaten track. In these cases, it is the home itself that brings issues of who lives where, and of how people live, so sharply into focus.

But we may discover other possibilities if we turn to the theatre building itself. If the theatre is a house, whose house is theatre? And what kind of house? To whom does theatre open its doors, and who still cannot gain access to this most social of art-forms? When performers in 1970s Lower Manhattan found they could no longer afford the rents on theatre spaces, they got around the problem of rising real estate prices by occupying 'found' spaces on a temporary basis. In some places in the world today, this is still an effective tactic. For example, in the southern Spanish city of Seville, where the economic crisis had hit hard, architect Santiago Cirugeda and theatre director Jorge Barroso occupied a plot of disused public land and built La Carpa, an independent arts space which, between 2010 and 2014, offered performances and workshops to tens of thousands of people. But context is all and, in other places, the politics of opening a temporary venue are fraught with contradiction. In London, the craze for pop-up venues has been incorporated so successfully within a mainstream logic of transience – temporary jobs, temporary housing, buy-it-now-it-may-be-gone-tomorrow experiences and other (not so) cheap thrills – that, ironically, the politically resistant move here might be to sit tight and refuse to budge from a permanent architectural base. And while we do so, might we not re-think what a theatre is, what it has to offer and what kinds of values we are modelling through our design of its auditorium and front- and back-of-house spaces?

In 1960s France, director Ariane Mnouchkine set up Théâtre du Soleil as a theatre cooperative whose members lived, worked and ate together at their found-space home at la Cartoucherie de Vincennes, on the fringes of Paris. Today, on the outskirts of Yogyakarta, Indonesia, members of Teater Garasi not only share their theatre commune with one another but also make space for workers from the neighbouring rice paddies and their children to come and watch the shows (or fall asleep at the side of the stage) for free. I do not want to suggest that the theatre should fulfil the proper function of the state in providing adequate shelter and facilities for those in need – it is not the theatre's job to do this, and any theatre seeking to ameliorate problems caused by lack of adequate provision could (unwittingly) prevent people from fighting for a more lasting and satisfactory solution. However, some theatre policies and approaches to theatre architecture might work well in this regard. For instance, we might think about extending past those few committed, non-commercial venues the principle of unreserved seating, which refuses to segregate people spatially according to wealth, or about increasing access and broadening audience demographics through pay-what-you-can nights, when low-income and unwaged people might enjoy the best seats in the house for a fraction of the ticket's full price. Architecturally, we might seek ways to express in built form how the theatre, like the residential house, is susceptible to market forces, planning constraints, changes of tenant and the amount of money available for maintenance at any given time. A theatre project that created the sorts of informal spaces that foster hospitality and social inclusivity while refusing to peddle social fantasies of the home or to repeat unthinkingly the contained, sequential spaces that are our bourgeois inheritance could challenge capitalism's model of the private dwelling and model a more convivial, shared sense of place – one that would link the theatre with certain other houses (e.g. coffeehouses, public houses) intended for sociality and debate.

In summary, thinking about the ways the artistic, ideological and social work done by theatre is partly produced by architecture helps us to see the latter as both site and set of tools for theatre to explore its modes of production, and to reach beyond its immediate disciplinary concerns to connect to broader cultural or politico-economic issues.

Theatre and the tectonic

Defining tectonics

If the previous section was partly genealogical and was aimed at tracing an explicitly architectural theatre history, my goal in this final section is mainly pedagogical. Here, I analyse and speculate about the possibility of shared methodologies between theatre and architecture. I ask: What might it mean to produce theatre by way of architecture? And in elaborating one possible answer to this question, I turn to tectonics, the branch of architecture that deals with the poetics of construction. If we imagine that theatre speaks to, learns from and, in other valuable ways, intersects with tectonic culture, we are likely to experience a subtle yet profound shift in the ways we think about and do it. So, let's take a more careful look at the topic.

Linked etymologically to the ancient Greek and Sanskrit words for carpentry, the tectonic has been closely associated with architecture since the mid-nineteenth century, when the concept was used to stimulate thinking about how to articulate the relationship between constructional form and material character, aligning structure and style. Tectonics is not a style or a movement; it is an approach, a way of working, which has many different manifestations, although these manifestations are characterised by a number of shared themes and concerns. Chief among these is the importance given to ensuring a satisfying relationship between a form (an organised whole), its structural force (the way its parts stand up and hold firm) and its symbolic potency (the conviction and flair with which it represents an idea, object or association). Tectonics is pragmatic yet imaginative, rooted in a sense of place as well as in corporeality, topography and multi-sensory perception, innovative in its use of the materials and technologies available to it and painstaking in its attention to craftsmanship and detailing.

Joseph Paxton's Crystal Palace (1851) provides a good example of the nineteenth-century tectonic, the lessons of which are still instructive. Built in London's Hyde Park to house the 'Great Exhibition of the Works of Industry of All Nations', the Crystal Palace used a revolutionary modular, prefabricated design that was at once brilliantly simple yet structurally novel and poetically rich. Every part of the finished form was self-supporting: nothing was extraneous and nothing was hidden, disguised or left unjustified in the overall composition. Materials, textures and structural elements visibly announced their nature and purpose, creating a series of dynamically contrasting inter-relationships. There was a real sense in which the exhibition hall itself could be read as a performance of British industrial and technological ingenuity (never mind the contents of the exhibition), since the Crystal Palace revelled in the poetic contrast it established between earthbound iron and translucent, sky-reaching glass. In all, Paxton's design was highly original, unswerving and honest in its co-ordination of structural, representational and contextual elements and bold in its provocation to other innovators to re-think principles of fabrication in relation to the properties of materials.

In contemporary architecture practice, the core values of the tectonic remain unchanged, although architects who are responding to traditional ideas and applications of the tectonic are expanding its basic principles in ways I believe could resonate as clearly for performance-makers and drama teachers as they do for the architecture and construction industries and their related schools and training centres. In *Radical Tectonics* (2001), Annette Lecuyer notes how the contemporary tectonic is extending the parameters of innovative craftsmanship beyond building type and topography to include discursive sites and social contexts, and is sparking renewed interest in the sensate and in the body's experience of space, form and location – concerns that parallel explorations of performance and place in contemporary theatre practice (pp. 18–19). Meanwhile, Tim Culvahouse argues that if the tectonic has always concerned the specifics of how a work comes to be collectively developed and realised, one of its main uses in a world of separate professional specialisms might be in ensuring productive working relations between the different players whose combined contributions are needed to produce the end result ('Book Review: Kenneth Frampton, *Studies in Tectonic Culture*', 1996, p. 11). In architecture practice, this is likely to mean re-thinking the ways that architects, clients, construction workers, local interest groups, planners, project managers and structural engineers interact with one another; in performance, it might lead to greater awareness of the nature of the various social and artistic inter-dependencies that exist between performers, scenographers, spectators, technicians and others involved in the event. In addition, as we develop new technologies and materials that enable us to construct previously unimaginable forms, we might see the twenty-first-century tectonic as offering a set of guiding principles by which we can mediate between the analogue and the digital, poetic and cognitive, thematic and formal aspects of a project – in architecture or performance. Indeed, as definitions and applications shift to keep pace with changing cultural contexts and different ways of making, the tectonic proves to be a flexible yet precise concept.

Dramaturgy and the poetics of construction

Why I think tectonics matters for theatre is because, over the past few decades, we have seen an explosion of new performance practices. And while the break with established theatrical traditions is exhilarating, it is important that emerging practitioners find optimal ways to exploit the unique features of their form or format – to make theatre that works. Viewing theatre in terms of the tectonic might remind us that while it is sometimes text-ile, it is always technical and tactile, since it is centred on the tangible materiality of performing bodies and/or objects. As in architecture, where the tectonic builds component parts in ways that are structurally sound and structurally expressive, related to context and circumstance, a tectonics of theatre might encourage us to think about how we craft a piece of work: What is holding it together, enabling its ideas to stand up? How might our chosen form rise above its role as mere carrier of content to act as a communicative force in its own right? What significance might be attributed to the combining, interweaving or juxtaposing of dramatic elements, textures and/or materials? How will we connect the different moments within the performance and facilitate the audience's transition between them? What connections might exist between the work and its physical, social, ideological and other contexts, and how will these be articulated through our bodies, our words, the space, light and sound?

In a sense, what I am talking about is a kind of dramaturgical activity – or, perhaps, a particular way of doing dramaturgy. However, I think it is worth making the point about a poetics of *construction* since dramaturgy in Europe and many other places is firmly associated with playwriting and the literary departments of (writers') theatres. As the systematic approach to shaping and strengthening a play-text or performance, dramaturgy provides creative support, contextual knowledge and constructive criticism that enhances the composition. Yet the evidence of many full-length publications on dramaturgy (e.g. Judith Rudakoff and Lynn M. Thomson, *Between the Lines: The Process of Dramaturgy*, 2002; Mary Luckhurst, *Dramaturgy: A Revolution in Theatre*, 2006), as well as descriptions of university dramaturgy modules in the UK and Europe, shows the emphasis falling more heavily on skills of writing, re-writing, translating, adapting, reading and decoding than it does on pushing the possibilities for formal inventiveness and for making theatre work through concrete circumstance, action, material, task and craft.

Some dramaturgs and theatre scholars are now expanding definitions of dramaturgy to take into account the complexity of emerging practices, many of which are not based in text or linear narrative. Performance scholar and site-specific practitioner Cathy Turner, working with dramaturg Synne Behrndt and on her own, has perhaps done most to promote the idea that dramaturgy is as an activity analogous to architecture. In *Dramaturgy and Performance* (2008), Turner and Behrndt note the use of assemblage – an artistic process in which 'found' objects or materials are assembled into three-dimensional structures – in the architectural dramaturgies of American neo-avant-gardists Robert

Wilson, Richard Foreman and The Wooster Group and argue that, in recent years, there has been a substantial increase in works by British artists, including Punchdrunk, Geraldine Pilgrim and Shunt, whose dramaturgies are rooted in spatial rather than chronological principles (p. 195). Turner develops this idea in her article 'Mis-guidance and Spatial Planning' (2010). Here, she uses architecture theory and practice (as well as spatial and political theory and cultural geography) to demonstrate how projects initiated by her performance group Wrights & Sites, including *Possible Forests* (Haldon Forest Park, near Exeter, UK, 2007) and *Misguided in Fribourg* (Belluard Bollwerk International Festival, Fribourg, Switzerland, 2008), can be read either as playful alternatives to urban planning processes or as examples of how architecture and the culture of the built environment are re-qualifying and energising performance.

I agree with Turner and Behrndt that architecture as a whole might help us towards an improved awareness of complex structures and textu(r)al and formal experimentation in performance. And while some discrete aspects of architecture have already enabled bold new ways of understanding drama and dance (e.g. Roland Barthes, 'Diderot, Brecht, Eisenstein', 1977, and Ruby Cohn, 'Sarah Kane: An Architect of Drama', 2001, who consider geometry and lines of force in play-texts by Brecht and Kane respectively; or William Forsythe, *Suspense*, 2008, who reimagines choreography in terms of objecthood and organisational principles), I believe the tectonic speaks most clearly to the theme of making. Because it has to do with joinery and assemblage (the term does not apply to metalwork or work in clay or glass in which materials melt or fuse together seamlessly, nor can it be used to describe random juxtaposition or eclecticism), tectonics helps us understand wholeness, integration and inter-relatedness but also fragmentation, rupture and critical un-building. Moreover, since its stress on 'constructedness' and our human potential to structure something has implications that extend from the creation of dramatic dénouements to the building of political systems, the tectonic supports socially or politically engaged performance. After all, showing how things are built, and how they may be taken apart and re-structured along different lines, is an essential first step in realising the non-inevitability of structures. The tectonic, then, has qualities to offer theatre that might aid the internal organisation of its parts and, equally, might strengthen the connections it forges as it investigates its own conditions of production and interrogates power relationships in the wider world.

There are many facets of theatre that could usefully be explored in a fuller discussion of the tectonics of dramaturgy and performance. I might well have chosen to pursue my theme in relation to playwriting since, as Gay McAuley reminds the reader of *Space in Performance* (1999), the 'etymology of the word "playwright" suggests not a writer, or composer but a builder of plays' (p. 36). To treat the play-text as an architectonic element in performance, as The Wooster Group does with its innovative formal arrangements of devised and improvised texts alongside deconstructed classics of the theatrical repertoire, is to augment its role and find ways of building up and knocking down our expectations of dramatic form, exposing its ideological foundations and its means of support. But in an age that has seen unprecedented numbers of performers taking to streets, public squares, former industrial sites and other 'as found' places of performance, a tectonics of site-specific theatre seems even more useful. Such an approach might help performance-makers achieve a sharper critical dialogue between place (topos), building type (typos) and the poetics of a piece's construction (tectonics) – three key elements in Frampton's view (*Studies in Tectonic Culture*, 1995). Furthermore, it might enable us to see parallels between the way a theatrical event is put together and the way things are engineered and hegemonies – dominant influences – are created in the world outside the theatre. But first: What is site-specific theatre? And what challenges does it face?

Site-specific theatre

'Site-specific theatre' is an umbrella term for a cluster of performance practices that are devised in response to the former industrial, institutional, recreational or other sites they use more or less 'as found'. This kind of theatre may work in tandem with, or in contrast to, its site of production. It may involve some or all of the following: processes of non-frontal staging, a dynamic approach to performer–spectator relationships and engagement with the history, location, cultural significance, function and physical features of the chosen site. Beyond that, definitions of site-specific theatre are both complex and contested.

Commentators have wondered whether the 'site' in site-specific practice should be rooted in a place or whether it might be mobile (as in the Los Angeles Poverty Department's re-staging of Robert F. Kennedy's original 'War on Poverty' tour around a 200-mile stretch of south-eastern Kentucky for *RFK in EKY*, 2004). They ask whether the parameters of the site must be immediately legible or whether a site could stretch to cover a vast network of places (as in Janis Balodis's *The Ghosts Trilogy*, 1997, where exploration of the uneasy relationships between colonial conquest, Aboriginal marking of the land and current patterns of immigration linked local sites and monuments in Australia to histories and issues in countries many thousands of miles away). Some wonder whether site-specific theatre need take place inside or at a man-made site or whether it might more fruitfully abandon built form and situate itself in relation to the natural landscape (as in the ecologically sensitive works of Brighton-based company Red Earth). Others seek ways in which to capture the collapsed space-times of the global present (as in Station House Opera's *Dissolved*, 2014, where video streaming merged people, objects and events in two geographically remote rooms into a single 'doubled' performance).

These questions, and the experimental practices they have prompted, are part of what makes site-specific theatre such a stimulating topic, and I have no desire to limit them. If the examples I supply in parentheses suggest the answer to these questions is always affirmative, the reality is that every site-specific project needs to be judged on its own merits. The success with which projects navigate meanings of site-specificity varies wildly: some manage to build a more coherent set of connections between site and performance than others.

There is no reason I should not elaborate my notion of a tectonics of site-specific theatre in relation to one of the complex, fluid practices listed above. However, I can think of three good reasons for doing so in relation to the architecture of a single, fixed site. First, a lot of site-specific theatre is building-based and fixed in one location (although it may well move about its building, use it against the grain of its intended purpose or gesture beyond it). Second, despite the high number of site-specific works being produced in, on or around buildings, explicitly architectural readings of site-specific theatre make up a far smaller proportion of the literature on this subject than understandings that privilege space and place (e.g. those drawing on archaeology, cartography, cultural and economic geography and psychogeography, ecology, social history, spatial theory and urban and suburban studies). Third, whenever I sense that a piece of site-specific theatre is not working as well as it might, what is not working about it almost always boils down to its architectonics – the sense it attempts to make of the architecture of its site and of its own composition.

As dramaturg Heidi Taylor remarks in 'Deep Dramaturgy: Excavating the Architecture of the Site-Specific Performance' (2004), it is not unusual to attend site-specific events where audience circulation routes through the space are awkward, changes to position and audience perspective seem gratuitous, and there is no reference to striking architectural features, little exploration of different axes, scales, textures or proportions, and no real sense of typology or building style (pp. 17–18). Ironically, as Taylor puts it: 'too many site-specific performances seem to battle with the architecture of their chosen site while stressing their spatiality and engaging in narratives of place' (p. 17). Given that the work's relationship to site affects all aspects of its composition – from dramaturgy and narrative to choreography and design, from its internal organisation to the metaphorical bridges it builds to sites outside itself, and from its aesthetics to the politics at work in its choice of site and use of space – there is a compelling case for re-thinking the tectonics of site-specific theatre. I end Part Two with an analysis of *Stifters Dinge* (*Stifter's Things*, 2012), a site-specific performance installation by the German composer and director Heiner Goebbels.

Building performance

Ambika P3, London, 2012. I descend a narrow flight of metal stairs into a cavernous civil engineering lab. An assemblage of pianos (upturned, their strings exposed), metal sheets, small mechanical objects and the wan branches of a few leafless trees sits waiting in the half-light. On the floor in front of this construction, three vast receptacles stretch out towards a steeply raked set of audience bleachers. On the far side of the lab, the luminous white from three fibreglass cubes bleeds out across the empty space; close by, a line of speakers – heads held erect over spindly metal legs – stands poised and alert. As we take our seats inside the subterranean vault, I become gradually aware of the intermittent jangling of metal and tapping on wood that interrupts the low hum of this stone-smelling space. The collection of objects itself seems to be producing these sounds and, from time to time, one part of the contraption in front of us shudders or twitches as it comes into contact with another. Before long, two stage hands appear. They fill the shallow vats with water (fed through tubes) from the glowing tanks. Once each container has been filled, they sprinkle white powder through giant sieves across the surface of the pools. Afterwards, they leave, and, for the remainder of the eighty-minute piece, we are left alone with this strange mechanical sculpture. There is no narrative. There are no human actors. At the climax of the piece, to the strains of some frenzied arpeggios, the waters begin to bubble and steam like some primordial geyser. The pianos glide ominously towards us and then, just as mysteriously, retreat back over the waters to where it all began.

   Stifters Dinge investigates the phenomena and agendas shaping our world, using an approach that I would say is substantially tectonic. The piece braids together the architecture of the 1960s lab and the sonic architecture of live and pre-recorded noises and voices (including those of civil rights activist Malcolm X, anthropologist Claude Lévi-Strauss and Beat Generation writer William Burroughs) with new media theatre and striking scenography to meditate on how we experience the junctures between the natural world and the worlds of industry, technology and politics. Three facets of *Stifters Dinge* occur to me as offering a new generation of theatre-makers especially keen insights into performance composition. These are Goebbels's working methods; the question of what the piece asks of, and gives to, its audiences; and the precise nature of its site-specificity. I argue that the richness of the work's meanings, the heightened role it gives audience members and the provocative use it makes of its site are effects of its tectonics – the poetic rigour of its construction.

Goebbels and his scenographer Klaus Grünberg developed the work collaboratively from a simple starting point: their curiosity about making a performance without performers, or a 'no-man show' (Goebbels, 'Processes of Devising Composed Theatre,' 2009). Following an initial workshop in which they improvised with water and a piano, they added elements one by one, building the piece up through hands-on experimentation (rather than preconception about the piece's meanings) and passing on the 'questions which are actually raised up by the material itself' (Goebbels, in conversation with John Schaefer on the radio programme *Soundtrack*, 2009). Such pragmatism is typical of a tectonic approach. It is important to stress that the selected elements are not arbitrary: they work, as in the tectonic of assemblage, in meaningful relationship to one another. In contrast to Wagner's notion of the ideal opera as a *Gesamtkunstwerk* – a seamless fusion of artforms – Goebbels says that his post-operatic music-theatre is 'defined by the separation of elements' needed to make it (Richard Moss, 'Artangel Goes Subterranean with Heiner Goebbels' *Stifters Dinge*', 2008). This creates an unusually open play of meanings in which, as Gelsey Bell notices, 'ethnographic recordings appear in the topography of the performance like the rain does, as an object or environmental process – an idea, a melody, a historical citation – that is put into material and poetic play' ('Driving Deeper into That Thing', 2010, p. 155). Through the restless organisation of its elements, the piece echoes Austrian Romantic writer Adalbert Stifter's obsessive meditations on 'thing-ness', and instigates a search for sense and purpose in things that continually pit the human against the non-human, and range from philosophical and meteorological systems to political and chemical structures. Throughout, the tectonic inheres as much in Goebbels's sensitivity to the relationship of one material or texture to another, to non-hierarchical flows of ideas and labour, and to the relationship between physical and discursive sites as it does in his use of Stifter's voice as a mechanism for holding together the various other components of the composition (Goebbels, 'Explain Nothing. Put It There. Say It. Leave', 2009).

In creating a series of dialectical relationships between industrial mechanisation and the natural landscape, human and object, European power and non-European 'Other', liveness and mediatisation, triumphal and destructive urges, Goebbels gestures towards meaning but never finally delivers. In fact, for all the right-angled austerity of its 14,000-square-foot installation space, and the straight-on arrangement of set and seating within it, the piece creates a strongly centripetal pull. The advantage of its decided undecidability and the vortex-like way it sucks in associations and memories (what we might call its mnemo-tectonics) from outside itself is that *Stifters Dinge* affords each audience member a compositional role. Having sat through this pleasurable assault on my senses, I felt it would be crass to ask my companion what he thought it meant. But I did hear several other people – equally bewildered by the experience – ask the question I eventually posed: What did you *make* of it?

For seven days during the 2012 London run, the audience's compositional role was heightened still further by *Stifters Dinge: The Unguided Tour*, which offered us the chance to wander through the space and inspect the workings of the mechanical structure while it performed a series of reprogrammed movements and random aural sequences. This new component muddied the lines between theatre, exhibition, installation and durational performance as well as between subject and object positions, shifting audience perspectives on the work and forcing us to ponder the relationship between the performance 'proper' and our experiences of this automated sonic landscape. It allowed us to view the work up close, to focus on details, and then to view it (and the other people viewing it) again from other viewpoints. In this way, it referenced the movement in 1960s sculpture from which site-specific theatre takes its name (Miwon Kwon, *One Place After Another: Site-Specific Art and Locational Identity*, 2002), while re-creating in spatial terms the experience of reading the meticulous descriptions in Stifter's prose, where nothing is assumed and everything is examined fully and as if for the first time.

For both the performance and the unguided tour of the installation, Goebbels sought out exact locations within the site for particular sounds – using the space itself to sculpt the sonic architecture. The marked directionality of the sound fed into the sense of P3 as an environment at variance with itself and underscored a poetic tension that existed between concrete bunker and wild, brooding landscape. This aspect of the piece's site-specificity is very much heightened when you consider P3's identity. The venue is a former concrete-testing facility and, although *Stifters Dinge* has been installed in a variety of other atmospheric venues worldwide, Goebbels is on record as saying that it was in P3 that his work seemed to him to be most resonant (Kate Connolly, 'When Pianos Attack', 2008; Moss, 'Artangel Goes Subterranean'). For me, this had much to do with the way it referenced its lab setting to trigger thoughts about which aspects of our lives are natural and which we have engineered. I see *Stifters Dinge* not only as a piece about nature and ecology but also as a testing and questioning of human constructs, including (through the ethnographic sound recordings and the Malcolm X excerpt) the construct of race. A further resonance and a contributing factor, perhaps, to Nicholas Ridout's sense that *Stifters Dinge* modulates between 'the heroic' and 'the apocalyptic' lies in the thought that P3 stands at once for human invention, for the ransacking of the natural environment and for the loss of jobs and skills as politico-economic interests shift and former industrial sites are rendered obsolete ('On the Work of Things', 2012, p. 392). (Is it coincidence that Goebbels chose Glaswegian actor Bill Patterson as the English-language 'voice' of Adalbert Stifter, a man writing about natural phenomena at a time when Scotland was leading the way in industrial engineering?)

Into this concrete space, where we marvel at extraordinary feats of engineering and quake at the thought of a post-human emptiness, Goebbels introduces the immaterial architectures of digital technology and light. Human beings and their environments act upon one another. Consequently, when we use new technologies – as when we build new architectural forms – we determine the sorts of organisms we will be. Space is now augmented, contracted, dispersed and made liquid by the interweaving of the immaterial realms. Yet the built environment exists as solid presence. As counterweight to the virtual and the electronic, the fabric of P3 formed part of an investigation into the effects of extensive mediatisation on human sensory perception, subjectivity and relatedness, highlighting the way our experience of the world today is filtered through these contrasting systems. *Stifters Dinge*, then, uses the proportions, textures and symbolism of its site, the set-up of material and immaterial objects and architectures within the space, the counterpoint of its two presentational modes (i.e. performance installation/unguided tour) and the very structure of its enquiry to layer a range of different yet related contexts. Working with what is available to it, it finds a format and a structure that fit its needs, and, cutting out irrelevance and distraction, it builds its themes purposively and poetically. In all, *Stifters Dinge* demonstrates how a tectonics of site-specific theatre might help students mediate and enrich the primacy given to space and place in site-based performance by reconsideration of the structural, constructional and symbolic work through which they are achieved.

Conclusion

There is one final point I want to make about the relationship of *Stifters Dinge* to its performance site. As Bell and Ridout also note, the set-up of performing and spectating areas inside P3 was oddly conventional. As audience members, we did not move around during the actual performance but, instead, sat quietly in our straight rows, looking at a scene that could have been taking place behind a proscenium arch. I wondered why, in all that free space, a director would choose such a static, conservative arrangement? The answer is, I think, two-fold. On the immediate level of the work's themes and motifs, the distinct division between performing assemblage and straight-on rows of audience underlined Stifter's interest in the confrontation with the unknown, in coming up against some*thing* and trying to comprehend it. On another level, I came to see the auditorium-like arrangement as a self-reflexive examination of the forms that theatre takes. By referencing the proscenium-arch format in the way it did, the installation issued a call to us to ask: What is (a) theatre now? What do we expect of it? What do we want it to be doing? And where do we see it going next? The fact that these questions apply equally to theatre and architecture provides one good reason that we should think these 'things' together.

Throughout this book, I have provided a study of each discipline through the conceptual framework of its 'other', in order to show how theatre and architecture can be productively thought together. Theatre and architecture enjoy a rich, complex and sometimes fraught relationship: in part, they are radically dissimilar (perhaps opposite) disciplines. Yet, as I have shown, they share overlaps of material, concern and practice that range from a focus on time and space to interests in the production, articulation and programming of space, in the structuring of action and event, in the construction and contestation of social relations and in the meeting between human bodies and the built forms they occupy. I have argued that theatre's techniques and methodologies might change how we understand and practise architecture and, conversely, that architecture as organising principle, material presence and compositional practice might transform how we see and do theatre. Furthermore, I have argued that it is possible not only to think about a politics of architecture in performance, or of performance in architecture, but also to think *through* each inter-section between these disciplines about larger issues that lie beyond them both.

further reading

Readers interested in theatre architecture will want to take a look at two accessible surveys: Richard and Helen Leacroft's *Theatre and Playhouse: An Illustrated Survey of Theatre Building from Ancient Greece to the Present Day* (London: Methuen, 1984) and Ronnie Mulryne and Margaret Shewring's *Making Space for Theatre: British Architecture and Theatre since 1958* (Stratford-upon-Avon: Mulryne & Shewring, 1995). The three volumes of Richard Brett's *Theatre Engineering and Architecture* (London: Theatrical Events, 2004) provide essays by industry professionals. Christopher Baugh's *Theatre, Performance and Technology: The Development of Scenography in the Twentieth Century* (Basingstoke, UK: Palgrave Macmillan, 2005) links developments in theatre technology, theatre architecture and scenography. Finally, Marvin Carlson's *Places of Performance: The Semiotics of Theatre Architecture* (Ithaca, NY: Cornell UP, 1989) and David Wiles's *A Short*

History of Western Performance Space (Cambridge: Cambridge UP, 2003) provide detailed critical accounts of (mainly) European and American theatre architectures. On account of their theoretical and historical rigour, these two books remain the most valuable works in the field. Both reference Peter Brook's *The Empty Space* (London: MacGibbon & Kee, 1968) as the key text stimulating interest in alternative performance venues.

Adorno, Theodor. *Aesthetic Theory.* [1970]. Trans. Robert Hullot-Kentor. London: Continuum, 2004.

————. 'Functionalism Today.' [1965]. *Oppositions* 17 (1979): 31–41.

Aristotle. *Poetics.* [*c.*330 BCE]. Trans. Malcolm Heath. London: Penguin, 1996.

Austin, John Langshaw. *How to Do Things with Words.* [1962]. Oxford: Clarendon, 1975.

Barthes, Roland. 'Diderot, Brecht, Eisenstein.' *Image / Music / Text.* Trans. Stephen Heath. London: Fontana, 1977. 69–78.

Bell, Gelsey. 'Driving Deeper into That Thing: The Humanity of Heiner Goebbels's *Stifters Dinge.*' *TDR: The Drama Review* 54.3 (2010): 150–58.

Bharata. *Natya Sastra.* Trans. Manomohan Ghosh. Calcutta: Asiatic Society of Bengal, 1951.

Boyer, M. Christine. *The City of Collective Memory: Its Historical Imagery and Architectural Entertainments.* Cambridge, MA: MIT Press, 1996.

Brand, Stewart. *How Buildings Learn: What Happens After They're Built.* London: Orion, 1994.

Brocklehurst, Robert John, and Juliet Rufford. 'Scratching BAC.' Prague: Prague Quadrennial of Performance Design and Space, 2011. Video short.

Butler, Judith. *Gender Trouble: Feminism and the Subversion of Identity.* London: Routledge, 1990.

Carlson, Marvin. 'H for House.' *Contemporary Theatre Review* 23.2 (2013): 29–31.

Cohn, Ruby. 'Sarah Kane: An Architect of Drama.' *Cycnos* 18.1 (2001): 39–49.

Connolly, Kate, 'When Pianos Attack.' *Guardian* 27 Mar. 2008. <http://www.theguardian.com/stage/2008/mar/27/theatre2>.

Copeau, Jacques. *Copeau: Texts on Theatre*. Trans. John Rudlin and Norman H. Paul. London: Routledge, 1990.

Craig, Edward Gordon. *Towards a New Theatre*. London: Dent, 1913.

Culvahouse, Tim. 'Book Review: Kenneth Frampton, *Studies in Tectonic Culture*.' *Tectonics Unbound*. Spec. issue of *ANY* 14 (1996): 11–12.

Derrida, Jacques. 'Signature, Event, Context.' *Limited Inc*. Evanston, IL: Northwestern UP, 1988. 1–23.

Deutsche, Rosalyn. *Evictions: Art and Spatial Politics*. Cambridge, MA: MIT Press, 1996.

Eyre, Richard. *National Service: Diary of a Decade at the National Theatre*. London: Bloomsbury, 2004.

Forsythe, William. *Suspense*. Ed. Markus Weisbeck. Zurich: Ursula Blickle Foundation, 2008.

Frampton, Kenneth. 'Rappel à l'Ordre: The Case for the Tectonic.' *Architectural Design* 60.3–4 (1990): 20–32.

———. *Studies in Tectonic Culture: Poetics of Construction in Nineteenth and Twentieth Century Architecture*. Cambridge, MA: MIT Press, 1995.

Goebbels, Heiner. 'Explain Nothing. Put It There. Say It. Leave.' 2009. <http://www.egs.edu/faculty/heiner-goebbels/videos/explain-nothing-put-it-there-say-it-leave/>. Video.

———. 'Processes of Devising Composed Theatre.' 2009. <http://www.egs.edu/faculty/heiner-goebbels/videos/processes-of-devising-composed-theatre/>. Video.

———. *Stifters Dinge*. ECM Records/SWR Baden-Baden, 2012. CD.

Hannah, Dorita. 'Black Box / Black Wi(n)dow: Architecture of the Void.' *PSi #14*. Copenhagen. 21 Aug. 2008. Keynote Address.

Hardt, Michael, and Antonio Negri. *Multitude: War and Democracy in the Age of Empire*. New York: Penguin, 2004.

Heidegger, Martin. 'Building, Dwelling, Thinking.' [1954]. *Poetry, Language, Thought*. Trans. Albert Hofstadter. New York: Harper & Row, 1971. 141–59.

Heynen, Hilde. *Architecture and Modernity: A Critique*. Cambridge, MA: MIT Press, 1999.

Hill, Jonathan. *Immaterial Architecture*. London: Routledge, 2006.

Jackson, Shannon. 'Tech Support: Labour in the Global Theatres of The Builders Association and Rimini Protokoll.' *Social Works: Performing Art, Supporting Publics*. London: Routledge, 2011. 144–81.

Jameson, Fredric. *Postmodernism, or, the Cultural Logic of Late Capitalism*. London: Verso, 1991.

Johnson, Dominic. *Theatre & the Visual*. Basingstoke, UK: Palgrave Macmillan, 2012.

Kelleher, Joe, and Nicholas Ridout, eds. *Contemporary Theatres in Europe*. London: Routledge, 2006.

Kolarevic, Branko. 'Towards the Performative in Architecture.' *Performative Architecture: Beyond Instrumentality*. Ed. Branko Kolarevic and Ali M. Malkawi. New York: Spon, 2005. 204–13.

Kurtz, Maurice. *Jacques Copeau: Biography of a Theatre*. Carbondale: Southern Illinois UP, 1999.

Kwon, Miwon. *One Place After Another: Site-Specific Art and Locational Identity*. Cambridge, MA: MIT Press, 2002.

Le Camus de Mézières, Nicolas. [1780]. *The Genius of Architecture; or, The Analogy of That Art with Our Sensations*. Trans. David Britt. Santa Monica, CA: Getty Centre, 1992.

Lecuyer, Annette. *Radical Tectonics*. London: Thames & Hudson, 2001.

Luckhurst, Mary. *Dramaturgy: A Revolution in Theatre*. Cambridge: Cambridge UP, 2006.

Maguire, Hugh. 'Victorian Theatre as Home from Home.' *Journal of Design History* 13.2 (2000): 107–21.

Marinetti, Filippo Tommaso. 'The Variety Theatre.' [1913]. *F.T. Marinetti: Critical Writings*. Ed. Günter Berghaus. Trans. Doug Thompson. New York: Farrar, Straus & Giroux, 2006. 185–92.

Marx, Karl, and Friedrich Engels. *Communist Manifesto*. [1848]. Ed. Gareth Stedman Jones. London: Penguin, 2002.

McAuley, Gay. *Space in Performance: Making Meaning in the Theatre*. Ann Arbor: U of Michigan P, 1999.

McKenzie, Jon. *Perform or Else: From Discipline to Performance*. London: Routledge, 2001.

McKinnie, Michael. *City Stages: Theatre and Urban Space in a Global City.* Toronto: U of Toronto P, 2007.

Miller, James. *Measures of Wisdom: Cosmic Dance in Classical and Christian Antiquity.* Toronto: U of Toronto P, 1986.

Moss, Richard. 'Artangel Goes Subterranean with Heiner Goebbels' *Stifters Dinge.*' *Culture 24.* 20 Feb. 2008. <http://www.culture24.org.uk/art/art54384>.

Pelletier, Louise. *Architecture in Words: Theatre, Language and the Sensuous Space of Architecture.* London: Routledge, 2006.

Plato. *The Republic.* Trans. Desmond Lee. London: Penguin, 2003.

Rahim, Ali. 'Performativity: Beyond Efficiency and Optimisation in Architecture.' *Performative Architecture: Beyond Instrumentality.* Ed. Branko Kolarevic and Ali M. Malkawi. New York: Spon, 2005. 178–92.

Read, Alan. 'Introduction: Addressing Architecture, Art and the Everyday.' *Architecturally Speaking: Practices of Art, Architecture and the Everyday.* Ed. Alan Read. London: Routledge, 2000. 1–6.

Ridout, Nicholas. 'On the Work of Things: Musical Production, Theatrical Labour, and the "General Intellect."' *Theatre Journal* 64.3 (2012): 389–408.

Rudakoff, Judith, and Lynn M. Thomson, eds. *Between the Lines: The Process of Dramaturgy.* Toronto: Playwrights Canada, 2002.

Rudlin, John. *Jacques Copeau.* Cambridge: Cambridge UP, 1986.

Salter, Chris. *Entangled: Technology and the Transformation of Performance.* Cambridge, MA: MIT Press, 2010.

Schaefer, John. 'Heiner Goebbels.' *Soundcheck.* WNYC, New York. 16 Dec. 2009. <http://soundcheck.wnyc.org/story/42977-heiner-goebbels/>. Audio.

Serlio, Sebastiano. *On Architecture: Volume One, Books I–V of Tutte l'Opere d'Architettura et Prospetiva.* Trans. Vaughan Hart and Peter Hicks. New Haven, CT: Yale UP, 2005.

Taylor, Heidi. 'Deep Dramaturgy: Excavating the Architecture of the Site-Specific Performance.' *Canadian Theatre Review* 119 (2004): 16–19.

Tschumi, Bernard. 'Architecture and Its Double.' [1978]. *Questions of Space.* London: Architectural Association, 1990. 62–77.

———. *Event Cities I.* Cambridge, MA: MIT Press, 1994.

————. *The Manhattan Transcripts*. London: Academy Editions, 1981.

————. 'Violence of Architecture.' [1982]. *Architecture and Disjunction*. Cambridge, MA: MIT Press, 1996. 121–40.

Turner, Cathy. 'Mis-guidance and Spatial Planning: Dramaturgies of Public Space.' *Contemporary Theatre Review* 20.2 (2010): 149–61.

Turner, Cathy, and Synne Behrndt. *Dramaturgy and Performance*. Basingstoke, UK: Palgrave Macmillan, 2008.

Vesely, Dalibor. *Architecture in the Age of Divided Representation: The Question of Creativity in the Shadow of Production*. Cambridge, MA: MIT Press, 2004.

Vitruvius [Marcus Vitruvius Pollio]. *Ten Books on Architecture*. Trans. Ingrid Rowland. Cambridge: Cambridge UP, 1999.

Wiles, David. *A Short History of Western Performance Space*. Cambridge: Cambridge UP, 2003.

Yoon, J. Meejin. 'Public Works: Projects at Play.' *Performance / Architecture*. Spec. issue of *Journal of Architectural Education* 61.4 (2008): 59–68.

index

acknowledgements

Many thanks to Jen Harvie and Dan Rebellato for commissioning this book and providing helpful comments on earlier drafts. Thanks, too, to colleagues and students at Queen Mary University of London, who, in various ways, have enabled me to think through these issues. I have benefited enormously from conversations with members of the International Federation for Theatre Research's Theatre Architecture Working Group and also from the constructive criticism of friends who gave their time to read my work. Jenni Burnell and colleagues at Palgrave Macmillan have been supportive, enthusiastic and patient. A special mention goes to the Palgrave Macmillan production team and, in particular, Jason Pearce, who worked closely with me to ensure the text would read as accurately and elegantly as possible. Finally, a big thank-you to my partner, Matteo, without whom this would not have been possible.